BASIC NEEDS

A Year with Street Kids in a City School

Second Edition

JULIE LANDSMAN

SCARECROWEDUCATION
Lanham, Maryland • Toronto • Oxford
2004

Published in the United States of America
by ScarecrowEducation
An imprint of The Rowman & Littlefield Publishing Group, Inc.
4501 Forbes Boulevard, Suite 200, Lanham, Maryland 20706
www.scarecroweducation.com

PO Box 317
Oxford
OX2 9RU, UK

British Library Cataloguing in Publication Information Available

Library of Congress Cataloging-in-Publication Data

Landsman, Julie.
    Basic needs : a year with street kids in a city school / Julie Landsman.—2nd ed.
        p.   cm.
    ISBN 1-57886-036-9 (pbk. : alk. paper)
        1. Problem children—Education (Secondary)—Minnesota—Minneapolis—
    Case studies.   2. Education, Urban—Minnesota—Minneapolis—Case studies.   I.
    Title.
    LC4802.5.M6 L36   2004
    371.93′0973—dc22   2003018115

©™ The paper used in this publication meets the minimum requirements of American National Standard for Information Sciences—Permanence of Paper for Printed Library Materials, ANSI/NISO Z39.48-1992.
Manufactured in the United States of America.

For Maury and Aaron,
who have given me my safe home

In memory of
Terrence Des Pres
Steven Orey
Duke Dubuque

CONTENTS

PREFACE

It has been ten years since this book was first published. I wish I could say that things have gotten better. I wish I could say that young people in trouble are receiving more help, more attention and more funding than a decade ago. I want so much to say that there is a new emphasis in this country on children, on education. I want to report that we are living in a time of governance based on true compassion. Yet, I cannot say this. Rather than a change for the better for our kids, recent developments in public policy have been devastating for teachers, day care workers, young people, seniors, the working poor and those who are on welfare. Even middle class families are feeling bereft as higher education is more and more out of reach for even those with decent incomes.

There is no question that in some areas we have seen enlightenment. In the area of diversity and multicultural education we are finding some fine new organizations like Rethinking Schools and Seeding Educational Equity and Diversity, that are helping all educators, business men, government workers and professionals as well as others understand the need for inclusive environments. In each state, in each city, in so many neighborhoods and small town coffee shops important work is being done to change lives for the better. Food shelves continue to be stocked and run efficiently in the quiet of the morning, in the long lines on Thanksgiving. Block clubs are finding ways to take back their streets, plant gardens, paint murals. Every day teachers are coming to work at dawn to meet with a student who is troubled, to hold a conference with a father who is concerned about his son, or simply to be there in case some young woman decides to tell her story in the privacy of one-on-one time. Principals walk the halls, calling out to students to get to class, addressing them by name and mentioning how well they performed in the talent show the day before. Lawyers are giving up their time to work with migrant workers when they need legal help. Doctors are organizing clinics in the city for those who have no health insurance. The list of Americans who care is endless.

And yet, this is not enough. As you engage in the lives of the kids in this book, I hope you will feel, as I do, that at the very least we owe it to young people to give them all a fair start, an equal shot at dreaming great dreams for their futures. This fair start is not happening now, and it was not happening ten years ago. Now, kids are still hungry as they arrive in the classroom, are still cold in the winter, are still unable to study because the electricity has been shut off in their homes. Some young people in our more affluent suburbs are lost and disillusioned, without a sense of community or meaning.

I have been all over the United States, speaking to those who work with kids in trouble, those who teach kids defined as "gifted," those who work with many students who do not speak English. I have spent evenings talking with teachers who want to do what is best for their students and because of the frustration of huge class sizes and weekends full of work, leave the profession because they cannot do the job as they feel it needs to be done. I have spent mornings with veteran teachers, like myself, who would not have chosen any other profession, but who are feeling tired, ready to retire. As I write this we are experiencing a teacher shortage. When this happens, individual children are abandoned, schools suffer in so many ways, and the Jimmys, the Jackies, the Sandys wander the halls trying to find someone who has time and space to talk with him or her. I am deeply concerned about this state of affairs. It seems to have grown out of a climate of greed, of fear and of denial. Greed as manifested in the rush to cut taxes and so deprive us of much needed basic services, fear as seen in the gated communities and the fight to keep streets and certain neighborhoods and schools filled with whites, and denial as expressed by many who believe, in spite of all the facts, that all children in this country start with the same opportunities. Or even worse, a new and powerful indifference seems to be prevalent as expressed by those who do not feel we must, as a nation, ensure that all our citizens have their *basic needs* met.

Another change, since *Basic Needs* came out, has been the availability of guns on our streets. This year, in a similar school, an incident with a knife depicted in this book, would more than likely have been an incident with a gun and would probably have had devastating results. As we have seen, this destruction has not been confined to inner city schools, but has occurred in its most costly form in suburban schools. Until we as a nation decide to face this head on, until our legislators become courageous in the face of the powerful lobbies, gun deaths among young and old will not diminish.

I can only hope, as people understand the gifts and talents of the young people in this book, and acknowledge the complexity and beauty of each life described in these pages, they will become advocates for a peaceful society, free of weapons. No one in our schools, on our streets, in our neighborhoods, sub-urbs, small towns is expendable. When we stop seeing people as representatives of groups and begin seeing them as unique individuals with a story, a culture and a brilliance all their own we will truly comprehend the lives that are being lost to violence, hunger and poverty.

Over this year, as my second book, *A White Teacher Talks about Race* (Scar-ecrowEducation, 2001), has been published, and I have had the chance to talk with young, middle aged and old people around the country on issues of inclu-sive classrooms, I have been privileged to meet courageous people. They strug-gle to bring literature, history, math and science to all students, in ways that encourage them to learn, to do well. These teachers are working despite great odds. They need our support. They need smaller class sizes, decent buildings in which to work, adequate funding for supplies for all students and recogni-tion when they do extraordinary things. This new edition of *Basic Needs: A Year with Street Kids in a City School* is for them, for their students, and for the parents who work to support their children each day, at jobs, in the schools and in the neighborhoods, on the streets, in the offices and all around the country. I wish them luck. I wish us all luck in the years to come. I hope, in ten years, there will be another edition of *Basic Needs,* one whose preface says we are close to our vision: an equal chance for all children to have a quality education.

Julie Landsman
Basic Needs: A Year with Street Kids in a City School
ScarecrowEducation, 2003

ACKNOWLEDGMENTS

Portions of this book appeared in a slightly different form in *Clinton Street Quarterly*, *Sing Heavenly Muse*, and *Hurricane Alice*. My appreciation goes to the editors of those publications.

I am grateful to the McKnight Foundation and the Minnesota State Arts Board for their generous fellowships when I needed them the most. Also, I wish to express my appreciation to the Loft, a Center for Writing, for their support over these years.

There have been many public school colleagues from whom I have learned what it means to be a teacher. Specifically, in the years that make up this book, I especially want to thank Tom Kitto, who has continued to be an important friend and mentor. I also want to express my gratitude to Mary Kaye Carlson, Bob Johnson, Mary Jo Coyle, Mae Gossett, C. Hanner Williams III, Iola Smith, E. J. Johnson, Darlene Franson, Jeane Dixon, Jeff Burk, Dave Andell, Tom Olson, Bruce Villebrun, Sandy Westby, Audrey Murray, Larry Zimmerman, Bob Lynch, and Joan Rudd.

Without the kids, their warm response, their tenacity in spite of great odds, I could not have survived as a teacher. Their determination has always inspired me immensely.

Without my fellow writers who have read and reread the earlier drafts of this book, I could not have survived as a writer: Jim Moore, Christian Davis, Pat Francisco, Sue O'Halloran, Olivia Galt, David Mura, Ellen Hawley, Shannon King, Jill Breckenridge, Mary Rockcastle, Alexs Pate, and Bart Schneider.

Thanks to the New Riverside Café on the West Bank, which provided me with great coffee and the perfect table by the window to write.

There are my teacher and reader friends who read a near-final draft and encouraged me to seek a publisher: Rosemary Prihoda-Pucci, Jill Lakowske, Paula Evans, Chris Thiem, Claudia Cady, my brother Boone Guyton Jr., and my sisters Lesley Guyton and Claudia Jones, and the Florida relatives, including my in-laws, Mitzi and Manny Landsman, Sol and Audrey Block, and Shelly Goldstein.

My friend Ruth Katz has simply always been there to read and offer support and helpful suggestions. John King has provided much computer assistance as well as never-ceasing encouragement. Lin Enger, who team teaches with me at the Arts High School, has never stopped believing in this book.

Natalie Goldberg gave me the process as well as the confidence and the belief in my own voice to keep going.

The late professor Harriet Sheridan taught me to write on the blackboard without turning my back on the class. For this skill I will be eternally in her debt.

I am grateful to Rhoda Weyr for her early support as an agent.

Emilie Buchwald, my editor, has been all a writer could wish for, and I believe the book has only been improved by her careful, tireless work.

My father, a writer, and my mother, a listener, have provided me with important role models.

Teachers who work with energy and devotion every day in the public schools under impossible conditions, in an increasingly violent and despairing world, continue to be my guides, my inspiration.

Finally, I wish to express my gratitude, love, and continuing appreciation for the encouragement, affection, and patience my husband Maury has given me over twenty-six years of a beautiful marriage. And to Aaron, my son, I can only say thank you for your hope and belief in me as a writer as well as your love for me as a mother.

INTRODUCTION

I have heard that once every seven years each cell in the human body is reconstructed. Because I have lived in Minnesota for almost twenty-four years, I believe that I have been rebuilt at least three times since moving here from the East Coast. My body feels, now, forever in tune with the landscape.

For awhile after we came to Minneapolis, I taught in the suburbs. I worked with learning-disabled and emotionally disturbed students. They came from trailer parks and small ranch-style houses, large mansions and condominiums. I liked them—the hyperactive kids who jumped around the building in pain after sitting too long, the quiet ones whose mothers ran the PTA, the one whose father was "born again" and who was kept so close and so tight his anger swelled under his skin.

And yet, all the time I taught in the suburbs I looked for a job in the cities. After three years I finally got the job I wanted in a special public school for students who had been removed from their neighborhood junior and senior high schools. These kids had assaulted staff members, often got into fights, swore at their teachers, and destroyed whole classrooms. In our program they were put into small classes and given individually designed instruction. They were also assigned to a group that met at the end of each day where they could work out their problems by planning ways to change and to adjust. I don't know how I knew that this was the place I wanted to teach, but when it came it was absolutely right for me.

The first year I worked with kids who were African American, Native American, and white. Many of my students couldn't read. Those who could read, read at the first- or second-grade level. Their backgrounds ran the gamut of possibilities. They came from homes where their mothers drifted in and out, occasionally fixing meals. They came from homes where both parents worked and together brought home barely enough money to feed their big families.

Often, their fathers were absent. Some fathers fenced stolen goods. From time to time their sons and daughters, my students, showed up outside my classroom door with watches, small radios, and jewelry that gleamed in the darkened shadows of the corridor. Yet I am convinced that these fathers meant well; they came to school from recent stints in prison to find out about their daughter's reading, their son's ability to use phonics. Their mothers were sometimes women bent on instilling the ways of the Lord into their sons, who had moved to Minneapolis from Chicago to keep their sons from the gangs. There were small and timid women who sat at conferences huddled under thin coats, pale from years of working at meaningless jobs in dry cleaners or fast-food restaurants. There were mothers elegant in fur who kept fine homes.

I learned about the differences in my kids' lives: their houses desolate or cluttered with knickknacks, their yards clean and bordered by perennials or littered with pieces of scrap metal, old car parts. At the same time I learned about the differences in my kids' ways of learning—what kept them from reading, what blocked certain letters and their associated sounds from coming through. Gradually I began to distinguish whether it was food, clothing, physical space, or psychic space they needed in order to be able to read. I also learned to understand and appreciate the sounds of black dialect, the hesitancy in the shape of Native American kids' speech, and the street bravado of the language used by white prostitutes who were my students.

As I write this, gangs have become part of Minneapolis school life. Beepers go off during geography, signaling seventh graders that it is time to make calls to their dealers. One evening recently, on the national news, I watched the funeral of a fifteen-year-old African American boy being buried in New York City. On the local news ten minutes later, I saw the funeral of another fifteen-year-old African American boy being buried in Minneapolis.

I grew up in a suburb an hour and a half by train from New York City, went to college near Boston, and later studied in Washington, D.C. The major difference I find between the cities of the East Coast and Minneapolis is the degree of severity of our problems. There are simply *more* kids dying in New York and Chicago. But they are dying here, too. They are hiding under bridges, cooking garbage-can leftovers with the old men and women who create homes in the most unexpected corners of the city. They are coming to school hungry, they are carrying knives, they are pushing their fathers off their bodies in the middle of the night, and they are carrying guns.

Jody, a boy I worked with in 1989 at a local junior high, began missing entire days, eventually not showing up at all, much to the dismay of his teachers, who had enjoyed teaching him and who believed he was doing well. One morning Cindy, the school social worker, and I went to his house to find out where he was and what he was doing during the day. He opened the door and stood before us in too-short pants, a ragged T-shirt, no socks, shoes flapping on his bare feet. It was the middle of November and cold. We could see his mother drift back and forth at the top of the stairs in her bathrobe. She refused to come down to talk to us. A baby girl lay curled between the feet of a couple of men who slept on the dining-room floor. Her diaper was obviously soiled.

We told Jody that he needed to come back to school. He looked at us, shook his head, shrugged his shoulders.

"I ain't got no clothes, man. I ain't got nothin' to wear."

"We'll get you something," said the social worker.

The next week, after collecting donations from the staff, Cindy took Jody shopping. They picked out a few sweaters, some socks, a pair of jeans, and a pair of name-brand athletic shoes, the most important part of his wardrobe. Cindy made sure Jody got free lunch as well as breakfast. When Jody came back he went to all of his classes. He missed only two days of school for the rest of the year.

One evening at a dinner party, not long after we had worked with Jody, I described his situation to an elegant woman on my right who lives twenty minutes away from Jody's house. She gives to liberal causes and reads newspapers each day, yet her response to my story was, "Hungry kids? In Minnesota? I find it hard to believe that we have that here." Her reaction did not shock me. I have heard it too often, more frequently here than in New York, D.C., Boston, Chicago, L.A., and other major cities. People in Minnesota refuse to admit that we do not take care of our hungry children, our disenchanted, cold, and shivering kids.

Because we have been praised for our education system and because we tell ourselves we have escaped the usual problems of big cities, we tend not to believe the bad news, the facts. The skepticism of those who are not faced with these realities contrasts sharply with the shrill hysteria of the voices of those of us who are. We who teach are silenced, almost believing that we *imagine* what happens in our rooms each morning. We almost doubt what we see: the advance of the knives and guns, the increasing violence, our kids stumbling into class hungry. We begin to think our urgency must be exaggerated, that we are being melodramatic.

We doubt until the next day at school, until the next afternoon when a young girl comes into the classroom and tells us that she's hiding out from her pimp, staying on the streets by the lake although it's getting cold. Then we know. We are telling the truth. Even here in Minneapolis, the kids are not doing well.

As I write this, a principal is recovering from being knocked unconscious when he tried to keep a group of Vice Lord gang members from coming into his high school. As I write, a boy who decided to stop selling crack and was beaten severely lies in the hospital. Our city, solidly midwestern in values, idyllically set in the midst of a series of beautiful lakes, is home to crack babies, runaways, and Disciples. We are not exempt.

This book is a recounting of a school year during the time I worked in a special program in the Minneapolis Public Schools, a program for students who are so assaultive and verbally disruptive that they cannot get an education in the regular classroom in their home school. I will call the program SAVE. Every incident described actually happened. The kids are based on real individuals, with names and details about them changed in order to assure their privacy. A few of them are composites of two or three students with whom I have worked. In order to present a situation in my personal life and my students' responses to it, I have collapsed several years into one.

I did not include the most dramatic events in my teaching life in this book. I did not include the death of Sherry from a shooting related to her drug use, or the gang fights in the hallways. I kept to the story of one class during one year. Now, many more students like the ones I describe in this book are in regular high schools in our city. Large numbers of them are not getting any extra help.

If there is one thing I have found over these years, it is that students like these want to learn. They want the tough love of programs geared toward working with them, encouraging them to read and study, making them responsible for their lives. They want teachers who will say to them: "You need to try to read, you need to learn this language, on this page, even though your mother was beaten by your father last night, even though your aunt fell down the stairs because she was so stoned she couldn't see. Here is food. Here is warmth."

AUGUST

"You have the baby, someone to love, someone
who'll love you, someone to talk to.
This was going to be my child. Nobody
could ever take him away from me.
So I made my decision to have my baby."

—Leticia, pregnant at 15,
from *Before Their Time: Four Generations*
of Teenage Mothers
by Joelle Sander

1

I am sitting in my classroom. It is a week before school officially opens. The building looks beautiful: the floors waxed, the windows washed. A squirrel stops by but only briefly on the branch outside my window. The silence in my room is different from the silence after a day of teaching. Then the kids' stories will still reverberate off the walls. Now, though, I feel a silence of separation, of rest deserved, of privacy.

Without knocking, Leah walks in. I haven't seen her for over a year, not since she left one May afternoon to have her baby. A couple of times last year, she brought her son to school. Then she disappeared entirely. Before leaving for the summer, I heard that Leah, at seventeen, was about to deliver her second child.

"Hey!"

"How are you?" I ask.

"Oh, tired, Landsman. Pretty tired. Did you hear?"

"No. Hear what?"

"My new baby died, Landsman."

I get up and put my arms around her. Holding her, I think about what I do not learn in the summer, what I do not know about the lives of them all.

"She was such a perfect one," Leah tells me now, her long arms on my shoulders, her face near mine. "She was a little girl, and I bought her clothes, a few pink things, so she'd be different from my other one."

And suddenly I know it all. I can see her bringing her baby home, laying her down to sleep in a small room at the back of the apartment, sitting on an old plastic-covered chair next to the crib, whispering to her daughter, the baby in a new pink nightgown.

And now, before school begins, in the moment when Leah holds me against her and the sound of her voice is full of bewildered sadness, resting near my ear, in my hair, now that we talk, I am not sure I am ready again for these stories, the anger, starting all over again, with a new group.

"I got to go," she says, pulling away. I put my arm around her waist, hers slips around mine, and we walk to the door.

"You going to school this fall?" I ask.

"Yeah," she answers. "Over across the North Side."

"You think you'll finish up?"

"Yeah. Maybe." She shrugs. "That algebra class is so hard, though. And that history stuff about Egypt. So much readin'."

"You're good at reading. Remember how you helped out Susan? You could *teach* reading!"

Leah looks surprised. "Naw, Landsman. I couldn't teach no readin'." She smiles, stops for a moment and looks side-ways at me. "I couldn't teach no readin'."

"Yes, you could. You were so patient with her and she wasn't easy."

Leah laughs. "Ooooh. She used to cuss everyone out!"

"You could hear her all the way across the lunchroom when she didn't like the food."

Leah chuckles again. "And then she would start tossing those trays all around. What she doin' now?"

"I think she went to Washburn. Somewhere to a regular school. She calmed down after a while."

"Yeah. With a grandma like that, you *had* to calm down." We both laugh, remembering Susan's grandmother, who had taken over the job of raising her when Susan's mother couldn't cope. Mrs. Walters would come right into my classroom swinging her purse at her granddaughter's head. Susan would duck, and I would try to intervene, but I could never get there in time. After one swing, she would stop, pull Susan out of the chair, and walk her down the hall to a little room where some shop equipment was kept. There they would meet with the head of the school for an impromptu guardian conference. For weeks afterwards Susan would behave in class, in the lunchroom, and even on the bus.

"She did learn to read before she left," says Leah, wistfully. "She really tried."

"Because you helped her," I say, turning to her. She looks pleased, accepts the compliment this time without a shrug.

"I really do got to go now," she says.

I nod, give her a hug again. I don't want her to leave, but she does, moving slowly down the hall, in her bulky post-pregnancy clothes, her feet in backless sandals flopping along the polished floors.

"Come back again and visit when the year starts," I shout after her.

"Maybe," she calls back without turning around.

SEPTEMBER

"The ultimate issue is whether Americans can be induced to care about children other than their own."

—Andrew Hacker,
in his *New York Times Book Review* of
Savage Inequalities, by Jonathan Kozol

A month later the walls of the high school building are already full of graffiti. Cigarette butts, broken glass, and overturned cans of pop that attract bees lay strewn around the southwest door where the smokers gather, early Monday morning. They are silent in the fluorescent light of the stairwell that makes me feel like I am under water. Inside, the kids in the halls, with their dreadlocks or spiked hair, are busy at their lockers in the crowded corridors. Some are kissing each other before the 7:30 bell. They talk party talk, small talk. I smell their perfume, their raspberry lip gloss.

Sarah runs down the hall to Algebra class. Just this morning she has gathered up all her clothes and run away from her pimp, frightened that he may follow. She glances behind her as she picks up speed, her high heels clicking on the wooden floors.

As I move down the hall, John Martin, a science teacher, stops me. He is standing outside the door of his overheated classroom. Sweat beads his upper lip. He gives me the name of a girl he is worried about.

"She cries every day," he says, "and she's always got her head down on her desk." Not many teachers notice the quiet ones.

I write her name on my list of kids who need some kind of help. There is no way I will be able to see everyone whose name is on my list. I know that, yet I write it down. If nothing else, I can pass the name along to the social worker. These lists are like some poems, never finished, simply abandoned.

My reading classes in SAVE are filled with kids from all over the city. These kids are in so much trouble in regular classes that they cannot learn. They disrupt the learning of others. They have destroyed many rooms in fits of uncontrollable temper. After enough of these incidents they are sent to our program, which is housed in a regular high school. Sometimes I have an hour with them, rarely two hours. By the end of the year some of them will have made enough progress to be allowed back into their neighborhood school.

At my classroom door, Sandy is waiting for me. She is angry because I am later than usual, although first hour doesn't start for another fifteen minutes. Her body slumps against the wall. She turns her face away from me.

" 'S'bout time you got here," she mumbles.

Our "honeymoon" has been over for a few weeks. She tests me each and every morning, first thing, before I have a chance to put down my books, slip off my coat, take my lunch to the refrigerator in the smoky, windowless lounge across the hall.

When the door swings open, she walks to the table in the middle of the room and settles her body into a chair. She keeps on her coat, holds her purse in her lap. Her back is to me as I arrange my desk and set up worksheets. I check the folders of the kids to make sure everything is ready.

One whole wall of my room is windows that look down on the playing field. Usually, this is the time of day when I gather myself together, but it is hard to draw breath when Sandy is here. It is hard to get ready for Johnny, Danny, and Mitchell. I want to drift, think about the weather or about nothing, think about the squirrel, again at my window.

I turn to Sandy.

"So, how's the niece these days?" I ask.

Without meaning to, she smiles.

"Just fine. She doin' just fine." But Sandy doesn't take off her coat. And her purse stays in her lap.

"I ain't doin' no work today," she says.

I knew that as soon as I saw her slumped against the wall.

Sandy's mother died when Sandy was eight years old. Her father left for Chicago and never came back. Her aunt Rhonda, who works for the telephone company, has raised Sandy and her sister Lisa for the past seven years. And now Rhonda is also raising Lisa's baby. In the evenings, on the phone, we both puzzle over Sandy's anger, her tantrums, the way she kicks chairs across the classroom when she gets frustrated. Rhonda buys Sandy elegant blouses and long skirts. She says her nieces must never wear pants. She tells me she is raising them "in the ways of the Lord," which means that they go to church every night and often on both weekend days. I remember my boarding school, the monotony of chapel every morning, prayers every evening, hours of church on Sunday. I remember incense and dark wood and the restlessness I felt, how I turned and twisted on the wooden pews.

I have told Rhonda how I feel about kids like Sandy: that they need hours to stare out the windows, that they need to wear slacks when they want to and to swear when the going gets rough. Whenever I tell her this, Rhonda sings hymns, right into the telephone. I listen. And when we say good-bye, she blesses me. Later, in bed, her hymn rocks me to sleep.

The first bell rings and the kids begin to wander in. Johnny Washington runs to his seat, talking the whole time. Every part of his body moves at once. He is small for fifteen, with rows of braids woven tight to his head. As always, his clothes are impeccable. He jumps up and kicks over a chair on his way to the pencil sharpener. He tells me that the bus driver shoots baskets with a bunch of kids before school. He's excited.

"I think I'm taller," he says.

"You ain't no taller," says Sandy. "You're still shorter than my cousin, and he only ten years old."

In a rare moment of self-control, Johnny Washington ignores Sandy's comment. He walks up to me and stands directly in front of my desk. He bends close, his hair smelling sweet.

He whispers, "See. My pants are too short. Don't that mean I'm gettin' taller?"

I whisper back, "It could be a sign, unless they shrank in the wash, or you got someone else's pants by mistake."

Johnny's face falls. He turns slowly, sits down hard in his seat, and throws a pencil across the room.

"Jus' had 'em washed," he says.

"Tol' you, little nigger," says Sandy.

Johnny jumps back up and moves toward Sandy. She stands towering over him. He yells up at her, "Fat-ass lard-butt!"

"That's enough, both of you!" I say, as I move quickly out of my seat and walk between them, breaking their eye contact. I search through Johnny's folder for a crossword puzzle. I know that he doesn't want to go any further with Sandy. Relieved, he takes the pencil I offer him. He glares under my arm at Sandy, who is still standing. Then he straightens his collar and carefully rolls up his sleeves, pressing each roll neatly and smoothly against his arm, one at a time. Sandy shakes her head as she watches him and slides back down in her chair.

Most days it seems that Johnny is strung like a wire, tight and vibrating. He has such difficulty sitting quietly, letting himself rest. In his previous school he was the center of chaos in classes of thirty students. His teachers always traced their bad days back to Johnny. Books flew across the room, pencils tumbled end over end, dangerously close to the eyes of shy girls in the back row. His failure to read even the simplest words was the source of mutual frustration; invariably he flipped over his desk or hit a student on the head with his textbook on his way back to his seat from the pencil sharpener.

His mother comes to conferences in the clothes of a model. She chews gum, presses the sides of her skirt with her ringed fingers. She has no idea what to do with Johnny. We don't know either and gladly take quiet moments like this one when we get them. Johnny fills in words on the puzzle, making large, childlike letters in each square.

Mitchell comes in, half awake, his hair standing in irregular lumps all over his head, his shirt buttoned wrong, his zipper undone just a little at the top below his beltless waist. He is not wearing socks. Mitchell is too thin; his ankles are bruised dark over the knob of bone that shows above his "high water" pants. He is fourteen and cannot read; he buries his head in his arms when confronted with sentences. His mother comes to us in carefully ironed cotton dresses and slippers. She tells us that she tries to instill the fear of God in Mitchell. We know she wants to keep him coming home in the evenings, out of trouble, but she doesn't always succeed. Mitchell has occasionally been found by the cops near a house not his own, his friends handing him tape recorders and jewelry out a downstairs window.

"Raggedy ass," mutters Sandy.

"Okay," I say, raising my voice. "No more."

Mitchell folds his arms and stares at his folder. A few more students rush in as the bell rings.

Davey walks in softly, choosing a seat away from the rest of the students, and gets to work immediately. This is his second day in my room, and we are still trying to show how well we can get along. I smile at him, touch his shoulder. I remember pictures of my own childhood, our family lined up for snapshots by the beach. My hair was almost white those summers, blondest in the family. Davey looks the way I looked, only prettier. I have heard that at his previous school he had days of uncontrollable tantrums and then days of total withdrawal. I know that in a few weeks he may display this anger in my room like the rest of them. But for now, he behaves perfectly. His best friend, Karen, a girl with pencil-thin legs and long greasy hair, pops her head in at the door. Davey waves her away. She has many bruises, the other teachers say. Her mother has a history of picking up and moving whenever someone notices. Karen "smokes like a fiend," they say. Now she smiles at me and I smile back.

Davey raises his hand to ask for my help. I sit by him for a moment, show him how to sound out three-syllable words. I ask him to read the first sentence of a short story I have found. He struggles with the words in a voice that is light and soft. He understands what he reads, and I leave him working intensely on the first paragraph, his lips forming each word.

I have never met Davey's mother or father. No one comes to conferences and there is no phone in his house. No one will open the door when we attempt to make home visits. I sense that he and his girlfriend Karen are on the run many nights. The social worker is trying to find out what their situation is. Davey seems grateful for the warmth of the school building on these increasingly chilly September mornings.

Sandy eases out of her coat, plants her feet on the floor, and opens her folder. She is quite formally dressed, in a blue silk blouse, gold earrings, a black skirt, and low black heels. She refuses to let me listen to her read aloud, but she does begin to fill in words on a worksheet. Once she settles down, Johnny concentrates on his puzzle and Mitchell fingers the flash cards in front of him.

First hour. Monday. Class has begun.

For the next ten minutes everyone works. I drift around the room, asking them to read to me, write for me. I bend over or sit next to them, our shoulders touching. The sunlight spreads across the room while outside the phys ed class plays softball.

The coordinator of SAVE, Ted Marvin, sticks his head in the door to ask how things are going. Fine, I say, and marvel at my luck. All the kids look studious. Fifteen minutes earlier he would have seen Johnny kick a chair over or throw a pencil.

"Man's head on a boy's body," mutters Sandy, after he has left.

"What?" Davey asks, looking up.

"He's so little, he's got a big ol' man's head on a boy's body," she repeats. Davey looks bewildered and goes back to his book.

Sandy catches my eye and smiles. Her face is wide and beautiful. For an instant the storm in her eyes lessens.

Sandy has a way of finding anyone's most vulnerable physical characteristic. Last week she said something about my breast size, something to the effect that if I turned sideways I'd disappear.

Mitchell has fallen asleep. His shirt rides halfway up his back as he rests his head on the table. I make a note to myself to have a conference with his mother soon. I can't seem to keep him awake for the whole hour. He twitches in his sleep, out cold. Outside, I can see a boy pick up the bats on the playing field. Johnny takes the last few minutes of class to shoot a crumpled up paper at the wastebasket. The rest of us figure out his percentage. Not bad—92 out of 128.

When the bell rings, Johnny gets up slowly, straightens his collar, shakes out his pants so that they fall just above the top of his shoes. He picks up his folder and sets it carefully in the rack on my desk. Then he rushes toward the door, his speed kicking in, his wire strung tight. He bumps into Davey, who, almost dreamlike, is drifting up to my desk.

"Hey, man!" says Johnny, angry for a moment, touchy. Davey smiles, waves his hand in dismissal. Johnny glares at him, then moves on past and into the hall.

I tap Mitchell on the shoulder to wake him up. He looks bewildered, but he gets up and stumbles past me. Sandy stands near my desk, unwilling to leave.

"Hate that old lady gym teacher," she says. "Makes me change."

I sympathize, remembering how my classmates and I stared at each other in the huge stall showers in junior high school. I remember wondering if my body would ever look like Sarah Williamson's body: large breasts and slim hips.

"Those are the rules," I say. "Now go ahead or you'll be late." I look deliberately down at my attendance book and she moves away reluctantly.

A moment later, as I stand in my doorway I can see Sandy's shape disappearing at the end of the corridor, her coat tight around her shoulders. I remember what Rhonda said about Sandy in one of our first conversations: "She's always been a tough little girl. She's always fightin' for herself or her little sister." Sandy's back is ramrod straight. She moves like royalty, unhurried, carrying herself with an exaggeratedly upright posture.

I slouched as a kid. My father would press my shoulders back and tell me not to sag, that I would never be attractive if I hunched over. Kids bump into Sandy and seem to bounce off her hardness. Yet, she seems suddenly vulnerable, as though she must maintain this rigid height because she is afraid of falling, of feeling.

My next class is one for depressed and suicidal kids. For part of the hour I run a group session, to let them talk. This is the second year I have been with them, so they are willing to open up. They talk about the dreams they have, dreams of jumping off high places. They talk to me of the desire to kill their fathers. One tells me that he is fine now, that ever since he tried to asphyxiate himself in the garage he realizes how many friends he has because they came to visit him in the hospital carrying white and blue flowers. He says that what he thought he'd lost is coming back: numbers and how they work, words and images, historical dates and places. These young men and women will often be hospitalized three times or more in a school year. My class is one where they can get caught up, begin again. After our group session I send them to the library to work on their first paper for Civics class.

Linda, who has listened quietly, stays behind, the only girl scheduled into my room this hour. She has blond hair and is too thin. She is wearing a pink sweater pulled tight over her small breasts. A locket in the shape of a heart rests on her pale skin.

After the boys have left she talks to me. She is pregnant with her father's child, the baby of some miserable afternoon this past summer when the air was humid. He came home early from work and found her in her halter top and shorts watching a game show on television. When he came in the door and saw her, she says that she knew what would happen. It had happened before. So she let him lower his body over her. She tells me that she had tried resisting him at night, tired but angry in the middle of a dream. She'd tried that, and it had caused a bruised hip, cracked back, and telltale purple over her eye.

She gave in without a struggle that afternoon. And as she talks, slow and tearstruck, I imagine the cicadas and children's voices outside her window, merciless in their wild noise. There was no time to run before he walked over to her, pulled the drink from her thin fingers and laid her out flat. She describes turning her head away from his breath, watching the game show. Afterwards her father pulled up his pants and wandered outdoors to sit on the front steps and smoke a cigarette.

Now, Linda lives across the city in a shelter for abused kids. She has her own room. She says that the food isn't bad at the home. It's easy to get her homework done there because everyone has to be in their room at nine, but she still gets angry at night. She talks about the trial coming up, her father, his anger. I touch Linda's shoulder. She does not flinch but looks at me and smiles.

The only time my father bent down over my body was in the middle of winter when he pulled quilts from the pile I had put over me because he noticed I was sweating in my sleep.

When the bell rings I ask Linda if she'd like to stay and talk, but she shakes her head. After she leaves I pick up the room. It is silent, finally, third hour, and I am alone.

I wish Linda had stayed. I know the courage it must have taken to speak this time, to say: "my father," "one summer afternoon . . ."

I stop in at the social worker's office to talk to Jane, who is knee-deep in paper. Three kids are waiting to see her. She has just hung up the phone after talking with a distraught parent trying to find her runaway daughter. We discuss Linda's situation. Jane knows the whole story. She is a person who knows all the stories. The stack of paperwork grows higher as we talk; a secretary puts tardy slips on her desk, a special education teacher drops off five due process folders, and a counselor leaves her six schedule changes to be looked over. She says that she'll try to see Linda again, make sure things are all right, ask her about the pregnancy.

"Oh, by the way, we're going to have a conference on a new student for your program," Jane says, searching through the crisscrossed pile of manila folders on a table next to her chair. Miraculously she finds the file she is looking for.

"Jackie Simmons," she reads and flips open the first page. "Pretty wild kid. In a few fights, driving the teachers at Sibley crazy, I guess. Can read okay, though."

I nod. I do not ask for more information because I have found I learn so little from paper, from scores or comments or behavior scales. After ten years in teaching, I have learned to trust my instincts and observations. I want only the most minimal data. I collect information in my own way, sitting next to the kids, listening to them as they talk and read, watching the way they shift in the chair.

Jane knows this about me. She is simply warning me about the conference. She is the best social worker I have ever worked with. She has common sense, energy, a motherliness that so many kids need. She is firm and warm, a fine combination.

I ask about her grandchildren. We talk about a peace march the next Sunday that we both plan to attend. We say a quick good-bye, and I make my way down to the lunchroom.

The kids in line shift their weight impatiently from sneakered foot to sneakered foot. The woman at the cash register questions each kid, fumbles over each name. Johnny, from first hour, stamps his foot, jabs at the list:

"Damn, lady! Every day you ask me! My name is Johnny Washington. I get free lunch. See, right there on the paper!"

He moves on, glaring at the flustered woman. Hmong and Native Americans gesture quietly at their names. Whites grin nervously and point. Some of the kids reach deep into pockets for change to buy extra milk or cartons of sweetened juice. Some take a bag of chips, forgetting the money they'd already spent on cigarettes that morning, then throw the bags back down on the counter.

One boy, Frankie, darts into line. No one tells him he "butted." The stitching shows on the bottom of his pants where he tried to sew them up, an old man's pants from an uncle now in prison. His shoes have no laces. He shuffles just to keep them on. He hunches over his food. None of the kids go near him.

Later, in my classroom, he talks about living in Mississippi, shooting animals for food. When I ask for an example of an analogy, he tells me that "coon just tastes like coon." The kids make fun of his clothes and laugh. He shadow boxes, moving around the room.

After the others have gone, he sits and talks. He tells me he can wax a floor better than anyone.

"I'm clean, too. My clothes, my skin. They clean, teacher."

And they are.

When the bell rings, he walks off, holding the waist of his pants, pushing his feet down the hall in the flapping shoes.

Frankie drifts in and out of school, in and out of my classroom. His father drifts in and out of jail, a quiet man who is often caught fencing stolen goods. Frankie can barely read the simplest words, struggling over consonants and short vowel sounds. I have heard that his father is back here now, out of prison, and that he is taking care of Frankie. I have heard that he went down south and got Frankie and brought him back to Minneapolis, determined to be a father for him. I have never heard a word about Frankie's mother.

In fifth hour, Johnny is back again. He has managed to get through the morning with his clothes still looking beautiful. He is one of the students assigned to me two hours a day for extra help in reading. At the end of the hour he asks me to read to him. The others like that idea, so I get out an article my father had published in *Yankee* magazine about a plane crash he survived years and years ago.

"Landsman, how'd he do that?" Johnny asks as I finish reading the article.

"Do what?" I ask.

"Do that?" he says, pointing to the picture of the crumpled airplane.

"She just read how he did it, dumbhead," one of the other kids says. "He crashed the plane and the erection seat didn't work."

"Ejection," I correct him.

"No. I don't mean the crash," Johnny answers. "I know about crashes. I see cars all the time like that. I mean how'd he get those words to be on that page like he wanted to say them? How'd he make it like he was talking and get his words so we could read them? Is he rich now?"

I try to explain about my father writing the story and then typing it, sitting up nights after work in his leather chair working at his desk after we had all gone to bed. Then I tell him how he rewrote his manuscript many times before sending it off to the magazine that published it. I tell him about printing presses and photographs and how they are reproduced and laid out.

Johnny smiles and says, "That's kind of magic, ain't it, Landsman?"

Magic. I thought that the fact that he lived when the plane hit the earth was magic. The crumpled heap of iron, the result of the wind that pulled the plane around: I thought that was magic. But words. I'd grown up with words. I had forgotten that magic.

Sixth hour, the last hour of the day. I spend it with Carl, who is sixteen. He so much wants to die, and I am not sure how to convince him to save himself. I keep him in front of me in his leather jacket, dirty jeans, and body shirt. His hair falls around his shoulders. He tells me he can't eat. He says that when he tries to read, the page goes white. When I ask him what he is proud of, he says, "my hair." He lifts it up and sets it on his shoulders. It is always clean.

When I ask him what one thing he would like to change, he says, "my past."

He wipes away stray tears, one after the other, and I say, "That's hard, Carl, wanting to change the one thing you can't."

He smiles and nods. He talks about his family having one less mouth to feed. He keeps lifting his clean hair up and over the collar of his black leather jacket, setting it around his face. Because his mother rarely touched him, he remembers an early morning in May at the park.

"She touched my face," he says. "She had gloves on."

He sets his own hair beside his face with tenderness. He talks about his jacket, all the zippers shining in the afternoon sun as the light changes position in the room. I want to ask him if he'd change this moment, now, easy tears, sunlight, the beauty of zippers, his AC/DC shirt, the memory of his mother, her woolen gloves touching his face.

I visited his house once last year. It is a small one-story house with a front porch filled with scraps of metal, old milk cartons, trash. I had driven Carl home and he asked me to come in. The living room was dark. I could barely make out dusty artificial flowers and pictures of the kids framed in gold plastic on top of the record player. An old beach towel draped the couch but the hole in the springs was visible through the flattened terry cloth. In the kitchen, Carl's mother paced back and forth in front of the doorway, her bathrobe opening to reveal a stained nightgown.

Carl had told me that stray cats were always walking behind the refrigerator. I saw a scrawny one ease against the wall and run down the littered steps to the basement. Carl followed my eyes, shrugged his shoulders. His mother barely responded when I introduced myself. Her hand was limp in mine. From the time Carl was nine he has had a paper route. All the money he makes he spends on food. His older brothers are often drunk. One of them was sleeping on the floor behind the dining room table that afternoon.

Carl talks about how he wanders down by the river alone some afternoons, or climbs across the railroad trestle, not sure when the next train is coming.

Suddenly he smiles. He tells me about last summer when he and his friend bought a keg and took it down beside the riverbank. They stayed there for three days. Old men, hoboes, ran out naked from the caves, put their heads under the spigot, and let the beer run on their bodies while Carl and his friend watched. At night the two boys built a small fire. Cars moved silently up above them across the Marshall Avenue bridge. During the day a motorcycle tore up the sand in front of them. This adventure is his fondest memory. And yet he is troubled by part of that experience.

"But even then, I didn't like the smell of my body," he says. "And my hair got dirty and stuck to my neck." He is not sure what he wants any longer. He talks about the river, about stooping over it to wash his face, and that the water seemed to come up toward him suddenly, seemed to surround his entire body. He says he was afraid that he would drown.

After an hour of talk and tears that fall unending down his face, I can't let him go. I call Jane, the social worker. She and the psychologist talk to him for a while after the last bell rings until he agrees to go to a mental health clinic. We are all worried that he won't make it through the night.

I sit alone in my classroom. The year ahead seems long, stretching out like the fields around this city, like the route the Mississippi River takes to New Orleans. There is so much despair in this room, and it stays, even after the noise from the kids at their lockers has died down, the insults traded for the day, and my students are on their way home. It stays, even after the teachers have left and Jed, the custodian, turns on his rock music and begins sweeping up the crumpled paper and sunflower seeds on the wooden floors.

It helps now to remember the small victories, the accomplishments. I think about Mark, whose father died two years before he came to me. He had not said his father's name since the funeral. Mark sat with me in this room in a small group, huddled around a table, talking about the lines on a job application. He always left the space that asks "name of father" blank, his eyes staring away from the paper. Everyone in the group was filling out the form again and again, so that no one would be afraid of a form when they went to apply for a job. When Mark came to "father," he skipped the space as usual. But then some wisp of a teenage girl with the thinnest legs in the world said to him, "Mark, you forgot to put in your father's name."

Without thinking, he wrote in the square. I didn't say anything, but he did. He said over and over, first softly and then loudly, "Logan, Logan, Logan." He grabbed a piece of paper and wrote his father's name and yelled it and sang it. I handed him chalk and he went to the chalkboard. He covered the board with a huge scrawl of Logans and then a hundred tiny Logans, singing it, saying it, and writing it. Because his back was to me I didn't see his tears until he turned around, triumphant, his lips moving, his hands covered with chalk dust.

A small girl with heavy bracelets said, "That's a nice name, Logan. That your father's name, huh?"

His mother called me at home that night. She said she had been trying to get Mark to say his father's name for two years.

Weeks later, Mark came to me after class to ask how to spell the word *deceased*.

I drive home through the alley, past the withered gardens and the empty places where pale bean plants began last spring.

When I get home, I smell peanut butter. Aaron, my fourteen-year-old son, has The Clash blaring from the stereo, and a trail of crumbs leads from the kitchen into the dining room, where he sits flipping through his math book.

Years ago I had vowed that when Aaron was the same age as the kids I teach I would try to work with a different grade level. There would be no way, I thought, that I could be with fourteen-year-olds all day at work and at home, too. But I am continually fascinated by Aaron at this age, by his integrity, by his ideas. Of course there are his erratic moods, his insistence on impossible freedoms. He is a night person, and I am not used to someone who comes alive at night. I have learned not to speak to him in the morning before he goes to school.

He smiles as I look into the room, and without a word from me he rises and turns down the music.

I run upstairs to change into sweatpants, a T-shirt, and running shoes. I do a few perfunctory stretches and head outside. We live three blocks from the Mississippi River, so I can run a three-and-a-half mile loop that takes me over two bridges. Running is the way I work out the day. I run it into the rhythm of my body. I think about the kids until they disappear. Today the leaves are turning, at various stages of color so that the river seems to change to gold, russet, or orange at each curve. After one mile I feel that I am only this water below me, only this body. After three miles I cross the second bridge and watch for my landmark, the same trestle where Carl spent his summer days. When I get to this part of the river, I turn away from it toward the house.

Aaron is asleep on the couch, the music still on. I shower quickly and wait for my husband, Maury, to come home. Right now I have some balance, my breathing comes evenly. When Maury walks in the door I do not tell him about Carl or Linda. I sit in our bedroom while he changes. Later, I'll reach for his arms.

In September, the students are constantly trying out ways to establish their places in the hierarchy of the classroom, of the school. Davey, the pretty blond boy in first hour, has become restless. He gets up unexpectedly and walks around the room, mumbling to himself.

Two weeks after Davey arrived, I found two police officers waiting at my door. As I struggled with the habitually malfunctioning lock, I nodded to them, and they followed me in, one smiling and picking up my briefcase full of books, lesson plans, and papers.

"We need to see one of your students, David Williams," said the less friendly one, his jaw tight, his thin face all business. "We'd like to wait in here so he won't see us," he said.

"What's he done?" I asked, nervous, getting out my books, setting them in random places on my desk.

"We just need to talk to him," the kinder one said.

"I'd rather you stood outside, or in the office," I said. I didn't want the kids to think I would help the cops trap them, that I was unequivocally on the side of the uniforms.

"What time does he usually come in?" he asked.

"In about ten minutes. At eight," I answered.

"Okay. We'll come back in fifteen," he said.

Once the kids were settled, the police returned. They stood blocking the door, the nice cop asking to see Davey, as though I hadn't already talked to them, as though I hadn't already taken part.

"Davey?" I called. He was sitting at the back of the room, his head bent over his book. When he looked up and saw the cops, panic crossed his face. He seemed deerlike to me, caught. He looked so slight between the two dark uniforms as they escorted him out.

A half hour later when Davey came back, he turned his chair toward the wall and refused to answer anyone's questions.

These days Davey focuses on Johnny, mocking his perfect clothes, his struggle with words, his excited questions. Johnny responds with jeers about Davey's thin T-shirts and torn sneakers.

Sandy is still keeping an immense distance from all of us. She comes in sleepy in the mornings after staying out late at church or after being up at night with her niece. She keeps her coat wrapped around her body all hour.

For weeks I have struggled to keep Mitchell awake. About the middle of each class his head moves slowly down onto his desk, and five minutes later he drifts off. I keep trying new things each day, and I sit next to him more often, nudge him, and talk in his ear. A week ago, one of the other teachers in the program was talking about Mitchell.

"I think the child's just plain hungry," she said. "He's not getting anything to eat in the mornings."

Yesterday we arranged to have a free breakfast for our students who qualified. Eighty-eight percent of them were eligible. Mitchell sat at the table eating waffles and sausages out of plastic containers. After everyone had eaten, there were five breakfasts left. Mitchell asked if he could have another one, and when the coordinator said that he could, Mitchell sat alone in the middle of the room eating a second and a third. I went to see where he was ten minutes into first hour. He turned to me, his chin covered with syrup. He smiled and asked if he could keep eating. I told him to come along soon, that he didn't want to be sick. It must have been my imagination, but it seemed as if a few minutes later when he walked in my door some of his scrawniness was already gone.

Today he eats two breakfasts, comes in on time, and works almost all hour, sleeping only during the last five minutes.

My quiet students are doing all right. Linda missed a few days, and now she has returned, no longer pregnant. She doesn't want to talk about the termination, and I don't press her. She brings homework, and since she and Carl seem to get along I let them work together. Carl was in the hospital for a week, and although he is out now, he is still teary. Yet he talks about rock concerts, things he's doing with friends. I watch him carefully. If anyone saw Carl on the street, what they would see is his acid rock veneer: sleeveless black T-shirt, mustache, long hair, and chains. They'd think him tough, no one to mess with, yet he is one of the gentlest people I've taught, almost elusive in his sadness. As with so many of these kids, his appearance is an attempt to throw us off track, an attempt to look like someone he is not.

Frankie continues to come to school, and his father is staying out of trouble these days. Frankie has learned how to pronounce one-syllable words with different vowel sounds that have consonant blends in the beginning, words like truck, stark, plop.

The weeks begin to take on their own rhythm. As it turns out, my first-hour class preoccupies me most of the time.

It is late afternoon. The end-of-September light still extends the day. Now, at three o'clock, the halls are quiet and sunny. All the kids have left for home. We are assembled in the teachers' lounge, which serves as a conference room when parents come to talk or when we hold meetings to determine whether a student will come to our program. Today we are scheduled to talk with Jackie Simmons and her mother. Jackie is the student Jane mentioned to me earlier in the month, the girl who was driving her teachers crazy at Sibley Junior High School.

Linda Golden, an art and English teacher, serves coffee to everyone, pouring the weak midwestern blend into Styrofoam cups. The social studies teacher, Mary Parker, who knows the kids' street lives, sees them in church some days, and is privy to news before most of us, sighs as she lowers herself into her chair. She whispers to me behind her hand, "I hear this girl is a wild one." She smiles, shakes her head. She likes the wild kids, can handle any of them, knows their families and what they do on the weekends.

Others straggle in, already eager for this to be over, yet curious, the way we always are about a new student. We try to gauge the ways in which the arrival of a new student will change the delicate balance we've built in our rooms, try to figure out which hour might be the best to add a new personality, which would be the worst.

As people reach for cups and begin to pass around the package of Oreos that Ted Marvin has tossed on the table, a small woman with carefully stenciled eyebrows, thickened lashes, and purple lipstick walks into the room. A blond-haired, freckle-faced young woman in a pink V-neck shirt, tight jeans, and a denim jacket walks slowly behind her. They look uncertain, not happy to be here.

"How do you do, Mrs. Simmons," says Ted, holding out his hand. The woman extends her purple nails, touches him lightly, and does not smile. She sits down. Her daughter sits next to her, pushing the top half of her body out defiantly. She takes a piece of gum out of her small black purse and puts it in her mouth. Her face is heart-shaped, her hair shiny and flat next to her slim neck. She looks strangely voluptuous despite her adolescent clothes. Her most striking feature is her large blue eyes. They reveal her youth.

Once Mrs. Simmons has accepted coffee and Jane and Ben, the counselor from Sibley, have arrived, the conference begins. All of us are alert now, no longer casual. This is a formal proceeding, a necessary legal and logical process. We are making a big decision: whether to take a child from her regular school and place her with us.

I watch Jackie as Ben reads a list of incidents leading up to this meeting. She stares straight ahead, the lines of her jaw tightening, her face expressionless. Her skin flushes slightly at times, then fades. Her foot moves to no rhythm, tapping intermittently.

It is quite a list. Since last winter Jackie has become more and more verbally and physically disruptive in and out of class. She is no longer allowed to ride the school bus because of three fights she got into in the middle of the aisle, at one point ripping the braid out of the head of another young woman. She has thrown books, pencils, and pop cans across her social studies classroom, has called teachers "fucking bitches," and has provoked many fights in the hallways. There are specifics, quotes, her exact swearwords. As these are read, a slight smile, almost imperceptible, curves her lips, softens her hard gaze. Her mother shifts her body away from Jackie while the counselor gives his report; she turns to the side, nervously picking at her nails.

I find myself wishing that her mother would change this position and line up with Jackie's body, that there would be two of them surrounded by all of us. As it is, Jackie is entirely and utterly alone here.

The list is familiar to us. In this room we have heard stories of kids who brought canisters of spray paint and covered their classmates and teachers with it. We sat through one meeting where a father admitted to trying to sell his own son for drug money. In a factual sense, this is not the most dramatic conference in which we have participated. We have heard much worse. And yet, watching the faces of the rest of the others in the program, I can see that they are aware, as I am, of a different kind of tension in the room: something more is happening right in front of us. This slim girl is poised on an edge, headed somewhere we can't determine.

I wait for the list to end, for the description to be over. When Ben is finished, there is silence for a moment. Ted Marvin asks Mrs. Simmons if she has anything to add, if she's having the same kind of problems at home. Jackie's mother stares out the window, her body turned away from all of us. It's getting late. Everyone is restless, shifting and shuffling papers.

"She don't give me much trouble. She just ain't around the house much. Sometimes, she is gone overnight. Can't do nothin' about it, though." Jackie stares out the window, totally unresponsive. She seems to have closed up as tight as she possibly can. Her shoulders hunch forward. She moves her eyes to the table.

"She's not a bad kid, though. Don't know where all the fightin' comes from," her mother adds, as an afterthought.

The conference continues. Jackie, when asked if she has anything to say, shakes her head at first but then speaks, almost as an afterthought, "I don't want to come to no different school."

"But we warned you," Ben says, leaning around to look at her. "We've talked to you about shaping up so you can stay at Sibley. But you kept fighting and swearing at teachers, even though we said this might happen."

Jackie sighs, puts her hand into her purse, and takes out another stick of gum.

"Don't you got nothin' to say?" asks her mother, nudging Jackie's shoulder. "Tell these people why you done all those things!"

Jackie gives her mother a look so full of anger yet so full of something else, too, fear maybe, or a kind of pleading, that we are silent in the face of it. We cannot name it. We only know that, as with so many of our kids, there are secrets at home, secrets that take place during all the hours we do not see them, during all the days they are not with us, that would explain some things, clarify our hunches.

Mrs. Simmons looks down, unable to connect with Jackie or with us.

Ted Marvin explains the program, its small classes, its regular group sessions at the end of each day in which students meet to talk about their problems. He asks if we have any questions to ask of Ben, Mrs. Simmons, or Jackie.

"How's your reading, Jackie?" I ask, trying to be matter-of-fact in the face of the emotional power of this meeting.

"It's fine. It's good. I don't have no trouble with long words."

"Good," I say. "If you come, you can help me with some of my students who need it." She looks at me for a moment, holds my gaze for a split second, then resumes her hard glare out the window. She's going to be tough, I think, just as Mary writes "tough one" on her paper and nudges my arm. I nod. And yet, I think, there is someone reachable here. But not easy. Definitely not easy. I didn't get into this program to work with easy kids, though. I got into it to work with the Sandys, Jackies, the Johnnys and Mitchells. At least for a while.

The meeting begins to wrap up. Others have few questions and little to say. Jackie is the kind of student for whom our program is designed. Finally, Ted agrees to accept her. Ben says he'll get the records to us and Mrs. Simmons nods her head in agreement at the decision. Jackie pushes back her chair. She is the only one standing.

"You can try and make me come to this fuckin' school, but I ain't gonna show up!" Her voice rises as she speaks. Her mother touches her arm. Jackie jerks her hand away.

"No fuckin' way. I'm not comin' here with all those roguish types." She pushes back on her chair until it falls over. She picks up her purse and turns sharply, walks out the door and into the silent hall. We can hear her footsteps as she runs away.

Mrs. Simmons stands up then and turns to leave.

"Thank you," she says, in a weak voice, her body and face soft for a moment, her smile nervous. She gathers up her own purse and leaves.

Ben says he'll talk to Jackie again. Ted arranges to have our bus put her on its route in two to three days. When we stand up to leave, it's 4:30, a hint of dusk in the graying sky we can see through the window. Yet it is still warm, there is still lots of daylight left. No one says much as we walk out of the empty building. These kinds of conferences are not unusual.

Jackie has hit a nerve with me. She has shown a kind of vulnerability I find disturbing. As I walk the aisles of the supermarket a few moments later, looking for a few last-minute groceries, I decide that actually none of these conferences is ordinary. If we are good at what we do, we will not get used to them. We will not get used to the way these kids look so alone at that conference table, to the muscles tightening along their necks.

One Thursday morning Sandy isn't waiting at my door as usual. I am surprised, but almost relieved. The solitude gives me a chance to plan some reading games for Mitchell, to think of some alternate way to get him to try to read.

The bell rings and the kids wander in. They sit at their places and get out their work without being told. After the second bell, Sandy arrives. She is dressed in the same white skirt and white blouse she wore the day before. She refuses to look at me or at anyone.

"You late," says Johnny, without raising his eyes from the paper he's working on.

"So?" Sandy stares at him.

"So, you late!" says Johnny, turning toward her, raising his voice. Immediately Mitchell's head hits the desk. Davey shuts his book.

"It's okay, Johnny, just get back to your work," I say.

Sandy turns away from Johnny. She sits in her seat and stares at me, widening her eyes.

I go over to her, reach for her folder.

She doesn't move. I place a worksheet in front of her. She continues to stare directly into my face. When I finish showing her the assignment she closes the folder and keeps her eyes on me.

"I ain't workin'."

"You don't get no points, then," says Johnny.

"She knows that," I say to Johnny. "You just get back to your work and I'll deal with Sandy."

"You won't deal with me 'cause I'm not workin'," she says.

Usually she talks about not working and when I ignore the talk, she opens up her folder and starts reading. Today, every muscle in her body is resistant. I can push her or I can leave her alone. I decide to let her be.

For the entire hour she stares at me. When I go over to work with Mitchell, I can feel her eyes on me. When I walk over to answer the intercom phone, I know she is watching me. She does not turn her body but only moves her head as I move. It is disconcerting. The other kids notice but do not comment. They are afraid she might shift her gaze and begin staring at them.

When the hour is almost over, I give the kids points for working during the class. They will carry this point slip for the rest of the day and present it to their group leader during sixth hour. Sandy earns five out of fifty points for bringing a pencil. She stands up when the bell rings and walks over to me. While the other students glance curiously and quickly at us as they leave the room, she tears up the point slip and lets the pieces fall on my desk.

At the end of the day, I learn from other teachers that she behaved the same way in their classes as she did in mine. I call Rhonda that evening to ask her if she has any clues. At first Rhonda can't think of anything that has been different in Sandy's life. Then, suddenly, she mentions, "She's been fasting for three days. Maybe that's what's wrong."

"Three days? Has she eaten anything?"

"Well, only what the church allows—a little bread, some water."

I remember that at age fourteen all I wanted to do was eat. My body was constantly begging for food, all day, every day.

"Rhonda, I think she needs more food than that to get through school. She had some serious problems today."

"Well . . ." Rhonda hesitates. I can hear Jasmine fussing in the background.

"How much longer is she supposed to do this?" I ask.

"Four more days."

"Could you let her eat more this evening? I think it would really help. I'm worried about her being able to stay in our program if she has too many days like this one." I have pulled my trump card. I know Rhonda doesn't want to go through all the meetings and paperwork of transferring Sandy to a different site.

"Okay," she says, exhausted. "I'll let her eat something."

The next morning Sandy comes to my room before the bell rings. She sits across from my desk.

"You call my aunt?" she asks, her coat still on, her voice loud. Yet she doesn't seem angry. It is almost imperceptible, but I can feel a slight loosening in her body.

"Yeah, I did. I was concerned about your behavior."

"She let me go out with my friend and get somethin'." Sandy smiles.

I smile back. "Good," I say.

"Yeah. It was," says Sandy, "mushroom and green pepper."

I laugh. She takes off her coat.

I have been waiting for Jackie to show up in my class. A week has gone by since we had our after-school conference with her and her mother. We decided to put Jackie in my first-hour class so that she can help Mitchell and Johnny with their reading when she isn't working on her own. But Jackie doesn't appear. Jane stops by my classroom to say that Jackie is on the run, that over the past weekend she disappeared from home and no one has seen her. Her mother has called the police.

This doesn't surprise me or Jane. The weather is relatively warm; it is still not hard to find places to sleep. And she was a kid who seemed poised, ready to go.

"Let me know if you hear anything," Jane says, "or if the kids say anything about where she is."

I put away the folder I have made for her and wait to see if she'll turn up some day soon.

OCTOBER

"The average age of runaways is 15,
their reasons for running away are more
severe [than previously], and fewer choose
to return home, . . ."

—from a National Association of Social Workers
nationwide study of runaway youths,
January 1992

Ted Marvin agrees to cover my afternoon classes while I take my first-hour students on a field trip to the zoo with John Martin's science class. I am rewarding my kids for beginning to settle down. Sandy has been writing short essays about her long-gone father in Chicago. She is working for points again and seems a little more comfortable. Johnny continues to jump around the room knocking over chairs or throwing pencils, but he's reading better and is not so obsessed about his height. And although Mitchell stumbles into class after breakfast, his shirt falling out of his beltless pants, he tries a little harder each day and stays awake the entire hour. Davey turns away from us toward the windows, yet he's trying to get through the book of short stories.

On the bus, the kids stay close to me for the hour-long ride. Johnny says to Mitchell: "That your raggedy ol' house over there?"

We are driving through a South Minneapolis neighborhood on our way to the freeway.

Mitchell grunts, "Yeah."

The house Johnny is talking about has a screen door hanging by one hinge, blowing in the October wind. The steps to the porch are crumbling, as is the paint on the entire house, large chunks of it gone, revealing a cracked yellow surface underneath. In the yard are broken plastic toys and old gasoline cans.

"Raggedy-ass house," Johnny mutters.

Mitchell remains silent. I pretend not to hear but plan to talk to Johnny alone, later.

The neighborhood is typical of this city: low houses, single stories, some wooden and some stucco. In the alleys, the garages lean into each other. Small children dart in and out behind trash cans and dogs pull at chains. These are deceptive streets. They do not look like the cities of the East Coast with their high rises and sunless rows of apartments. They are neighborhoods, yet the cold bite of poverty is here, the arctic wind blowing in around the windows in the kitchens.

When the bus pulls into the countryside, I notice that colors have deepened to red and burnt orange. The blond fields ripple into waves of light and the breeze is not yet bitter with November chill.

After awhile, almost everyone on the bus becomes quiet. Davey has fallen asleep in the corner of his seat. Sandy has managed to get a seat by herself. She keeps her face turned away from the others, watching out the window. Johnny and Mitchell whisper to each other and then fall silent. Some of the girls from John's class apply makeup. They smile at Johnny. They think he is cute. He shrugs. He is wearing a fur-collared coat I've never seen before and new baggy wool pants. A boy reads a copy of *The Diary of Anne Frank.* Cars pass us, and from our height I can see couples lighting cigarettes for each other and a single man in a suit speaking into a tape recorder as he drives.

When we get to the zoo, I let my kids split up. Sandy and Johnny stay with me. The rest charge off: first to eat junk food, then to smoke in the bathroom, then to see a few animals. Johnny and Sandy and I go to the water show. We watch dolphins jump through the light, through the sky, through the sun, to catch fish. They swim under a trainer in the pool and ease him up into the blue air. After the show we go to the place of night animals. We are down under the earth and our eyes need to adjust. In the green light, we see gophers and moles moving around their dirt homes.

Small children are running around between us, darting away from their frantic mothers. I do not immediately notice how quiet Sandy and Johnny have become. Sandy edges closer to me. I talk on, pointing out the different shapes of the burrows, the way animal eyes look like red lights in the darkness. Johnny doesn't say a word.

As we stand in front of a window behind which a gopher lives I feel Sandy's hand reaching for mine. At the same moment Johnny grabs my other hand. Neither of them speaks. While we move through the room, stopping at each window, I chatter on, amazed to feel their warm hands in mine. They clutch me, silent. They swallow loudly.

As soon as we reach the light, they drop my hands. Sandy pulls me aside, "Don't you tell no one I grabbed hold of you," she says in a menacing voice. I nod my head. She has no idea that Johnny was holding my other hand the whole time.

Johnny just smiles at me when we walk out to where the lions are pacing the hilly field behind the fence. He has been with me long enough to know I wouldn't tell anyone that he had grabbed my hand. I have something on Sandy now: something tender but secret. There is nothing I can say to reassure her. That will come with time.

Johnny runs back and reaches for my hand to drag me toward a pure white polar bear.

"Landsman, you got to see this honkie bear!" he says. He pulls back his hand quickly when he sees Sandy's angry face.

I turn to follow him, hearing her mumble behind me, "Yeah, Honkie. Go see the honkie bear!" She sits down on a bench and waits there alone for an hour until we are ready to leave.

A week after our trip to the zoo, the kids hold a dancing contest. Mitchell comes in the morning of the contest smelling of urine. He missed breakfast and in class first hour his head drops, then rises. He wants to read but can't stay awake.

I notice that Mitchell is wearing a velvet-trimmed jacket and baggy pants pulled in at the waist in order to keep them on. The kids are looking at him expectantly. For the first time Davey doesn't tease him about his clothes. Johnny whispers in his ear, watches him intently.

After classes are over, the fifty-four students in the program gather in my classroom. The chairs are pushed back against the wall to make plenty of open floor space. When the music starts, Mitchell takes off his jacket and places it on the back of a chair. He rolls up his sleeves and starts to dance. His whole body moves at once. His hands push the space around him into curves. His feet are snakes. Head back, eyes closed, he moves. A change in the beat provokes a change in his step. He pulls the music with him. He pushes it away. He gets down on the floor and swivels on his hips.

The strutters, the taunters, and the teasers edge off the floor. The well-dressed, straight-legged, jheri-curled kids move toward the walls, watching as Mitchell moves his hips, hands, and feet around the music. He is unaware of their shining eyes, their shaking heads, their "amens" of approval.

Finally, Trent, the toughest, shouts, "Go, Mitchell! Take it with you!" and then Mitchell smiles, as he takes the music inside, down and around his skinny body.

After that day, something is different. Mitchell walks straighter, dances in the middle of class when he finally reads a book, and stays awake for the entire hour. He sings songs in the hall, his church voice clear as a bell in the morning. Johnny and Sandy and Davey smile as they bend over their work, listening to his songs.

When Mitchell's mother, Mrs. Davis, comes to see me about a week after the contest, I am correcting the papers of my first-hour students. A large gray sweater is pulled down over her dress. She breathes heavily with the strain of climbing three flights of stairs. I put out my hand and she encloses it in hers. She smiles.

"Just checkin' on Mitch," she says, seating herself across from me. "Left my daughter in charge of the house so I could come over here."

"Mitchell is doing well, now that he's awake in class," I say. "We've got him on the breakfast program."

"He told me. That's good, that's good. He gets up too late to eat before the bus. So that's a good thing, that breakfast. I'm keepin' him in the house now, too. He got to runnin' around too much this summer. Couldn't settle down in school."

"I'm trying to get him to read more," I say, showing her some worksheets and a book from his folder.

"I know that!" she smiles at me. "You do want these children to be readin'!" I smile back. Audrey Davis and I have been working together for two years now, pushing Mitchell to stop fighting and to learn to read. When I first met Audrey she frightened me by barging into my classroom, picking Mitchell up by his collar and dragging him out into the hallway, hitting him on the head with a rolled-up newspaper the whole time. The kids said she did the same thing once in front of all Mitchell's friends at the roller rink. "She just snatched his old lazy butt out the crowd and took care of business," said Johnny, his eyes wide the next Monday when I had mused out loud about Mitchell's absence.

Another day last year, when Ted Marvin called to let her know that Mitchell was involved in a fight on the playing field, she showed up in his office, where he was sitting with Mitch, about twenty minutes after his call. When he saw her, Ted said, Mitch's eyes grew large and he jumped up and began running around the desk trying to keep something between himself and his mother. Audrey followed after him, smacked him once on his head, and then they sat down together to talk about Mitchell's suspension. Since then, Mitch has never been in a fight. And while I find it hard to watch scenes like the ones I've seen between Audrey and her son, I appreciate how much she cares about him. She pays the bus fare and finds child care for her other kids so that she can visit our program at least once a month. Even Johnny has a hint of appreciation in his voice when he describes Mitchell's mother. "She goes after her kids, Landsman, she don't take no shit!"

Audrey fingers the flash cards Mitch is working on, then flips through his book. "He's not gettin' in any fights, is he?"

"None," I say. "And after the dancing contest last week, he's doing a lot better. The other kids don't tease him or pick at him as they used to."

Audrey smiles again and relaxes in the chair. "That's one good thing, then. My other ones got problems, and I don't know what to do with Thomas, my oldest. He's dropped out of South Central High School and just got fired from his job at the Super Valu. I tell you, he's in a nasty mood."

"I think Mitchell is going to have a fine year, so you don't have to worry about him."

"Yeah. I'm glad about that. I just thought when I brought them up here from Gary, they'd settle down, you know."

I nod my head. Although I don't know, not really. I haven't had to move and leave my friends for the sake of my children, and I haven't had to raise four kids all by myself.

Audrey gets up slowly. She shakes my hand again and tells me to call her if there are problems. She heads down the hall to talk to Bart, Mitchell's math teacher. Each month she makes the rounds. Mtichell brings home weekly reports, as well as daily point slips and notes from us. But Audrey Davis believes in sitting across from you, believes in looking at you when she talks, believes in getting the truth.

On the last day of October, John Martin, dressed as a skeleton for Halloween, tells me that Mitchell walked up to him the other day and put his arms around his neck. This in itself is not unusual. John has always had a way of inviting touch from his students who want to be touched, and Mitchell can be affectionate. Mitchell stayed there for a moment in a long hug while the kids moved around the two of them, coming and leaving the room, waving passes in front of John's face. Finally Mitchell whispered in John's ear, quietly but as clearly as possible, "Hey, Martin, I don't know what the fuck is goin' on in this class!"

John and I both laughed, and I am still smiling at the image of Mitchell, his long brown arms next to John's pink face, successfully finding the right words.

Sandy is waiting at my door as usual. She's still testing me most days, still pushing. Yesterday, she threw a stopwatch across the table when I began timing her on a word list. Today though, she sits up, takes off her coat, and adjusts the shoulder pads under her new gray blouse.

I relax.

"How'd you learn about sex?" she asks me.

I am startled.

"Someone told me," I say.

"Who?" she asks.

"A girl I knew," I answer. There is silence. I think back to Cindy Strickland, the girl who told me. She lived in a tumbled-down house on the other side of town.

In Cindy's yard we gathered apples from the ground, set them in an iron contraption, crushed them, and drank their juice. We stepped over boards with nails sticking out of them, played around old cars, and sat on the cracked seats, afraid to breathe. Some days, I'd crouch behind the tilted garage and wait for Cindy to duck down next to me in the crazy grass that grew to the waist of the apple trees.

One afternoon Cindy told me about her brother's penis. She told me that he put it into her. She said that first he "did it" in a jar, then he "did it" inside her. In the Stricklands' yard, miles from my mother's rooms, what Cindy told me was just something poor people did. I thought then that sex must be like crushing apples: an act with no feeling.

"How did you find out?" I ask Sandy.

"What?" She jumps.

"How did you find out about sex?"

"My girlfriend Karen told me," she says. We smile at each other.

"But no one tol' my sister nothin', and she went and had a baby."

"She didn't know?" I ask.

"She's only fourteen," says Sandy.

I'm surprised but try not to show it. I'd always thought that her sister, Lisa, was quite a bit older than Sandy.

Again there is silence as Sandy bends over her book.

I remember when I was fourteen. I rode all over Wood-bridge in a two-tone green Chevrolet with Bart Simonson's arm around my shoulder. We drove up the driveway together where my parents' friends sat beside the tennis court, dressed in white shorts and white skirts. My father's head swiveled around to look at the way I snuggled on the front seat, my hip against the hairs on Bart's leg.

Later, my father paced the kitchen and threw his arms into the air. I sat on a chair near the telephone table where mother's recipe books were lined up in a neat row. He walked back and forth with long steps.

He said I looked like any cheap tramp from the "flats." I smiled to myself and wanted to chew gum loud in his ear.

"My parents never told me anything," I say.

"My aunt jus' say to stay away from the boys. That's all she ever say."

"My mother only told me to wait 'til I was married." I can picture the pamphlets about chastity Mom left on the book-shelf near my pillow. Sandy stares at me until I look down at my papers. She goes back to her book.

School buses pull up outside like orange dinosaurs, their headlights golden eyes.

Sandy's lips move as she reads. She is concentrating fiercely. I want to ask her to read aloud to me. There is no one in the room, and we could struggle with words in private. But I know that it is not time yet. Despite the way she's set, feet flat on the floor, the contents of her folder taking up the entire table, I know that she is not ready. Years ago, when I first began teaching, I would have tried to force her. Now I wait her out. I notice that she is beginning to change in small ways. She turns her body toward Mitchell when he speaks. She is clearly listening to Davey read aloud. She laughs at Johnny when he acts out a part in a play.

Whenever I talk to Rhonda I tell her that Sandy is getting ready to read to me. Rhonda laughs, a musical laugh, unexpectedly sensual.

"I know, Julie. It's comin' around to her time."

Sandy looks up, catches me watching her.

"What you lookin' at?" she says, without the usual hostility.

"You," I say. "You're really working hard lately."

Sandy shrugs her shoulders, pulls in again, closes up.

The bell rings. The morning moves along. Nothing is different or dramatic, but this time feels peaceful.

As I walk out of school this afternoon I feel that the day has been one of those plateau days, the kind that leave you with some energy. I see a familiar figure standing on the corner near the school. At first I am not sure who it is, but as soon as she reaches in her purse for gum I recognize Jackie; her blond hair is flat and damp looking, the jeans dirty, and the T-shirt unwashed underneath the jean jacket. Instead of gum, though, she brings out a pack of Marlboros, slips one into her hand, and searches for matches. She lights up, her purse slung back over her shoulder. I walk toward her, waving as I get closer.

The day is blustery, the wind picking up bits of paper and debris that litter the ground near our school. Jackie squints, trying to recognize me. She seems indifferent when my identity dawns on her. There is no reason for her to return my greeting; we haven't begun working together yet.

"Where've you been?" I ask. "I thought you were starting my class."

"Busy. Just busy," she says, inhaling and staring across the street in the direction of a condemned house, the windows boarded up with plywood, a door slanting on its hinges, blowing in the breeze.

"You at home now? We heard you were on the run."

"Yeah. I'm startin' back with my mom tonight." She looks at me for a moment, shrugs her shoulders, looks away.

"I've got you scheduled for first hour with me," I say, being factual.

"Yeah. I got to get in there," she says. "I been trying to decide."

"Come and see what it's like."

"Okay." She takes another drag on her cigarette.

"See you tomorrow?"

"Maybe. Tomorrow's Friday. I don't usually go to school on Fridays."

"Just come for a day, this week. You've been out so long already." I touch her shoulder. "See you tomorrow. You need a ride anywhere?"

"No thanks," she says. "My friend is coming for me."

"Okay. Take care, then." She smiles, just barely, her eyes, for an instant, losing that vacant hard look.

"See you."

When I get home the dog twirls in circles as she does every afternoon when she sees me. I let her out, put thawed meat back into the refrigerator, and change for my run. When I stop by the bathroom for water I see the electric hair clippers left out on the counter. I wonder what Aaron has done this time. He has tried dying his hair orange, but it didn't take. He wears high-top sneakers and striped pants with flowered shirts. Maury and I want closeness with him. Hair, earring, and erratic clothes are not worth losing him over. I change for my run.

After a good three and a half miles around the river path, I decide to slow down and walk the few blocks back toward our house. Four houses away, I can hear the music coming from our windows. When I step inside, I see Aaron's half-bald head bent over his homework. I think of not reacting at all, but that would be dishonest and unbelievable.

"Your hair!" I say.

He smiles, his smile, like mine, taking over his eyes, his face.

"Yeah. I shaved it."

"Only half?" I ask.

"Yeah." He turns back to his work.

NOVEMBER

"We would be doing a lot . . . . if we could help stop the hurting of children."

—Catherine Foster Alter, member, Carnegie Council on Children, *Small Futures*

Another few weeks go by. Jackie doesn't show up, and her mother says she is coming and going from the house again. When I try to reach students like Jackie, I feel especially grateful for the students who remain constant, who come every day, like Sandy and Johnny and Mitchell. Their progress is clear.

Sandy relaxes into her chair, finishing worksheet after worksheet. She talks about her niece, Jasmine, who now sleeps through the night.

And Johnny has been easier to work with since my visit to his house to talk to his mother, Marcella Washington. She met me at the door, ushered me into her immaculate living room, and offered me coffee. We sat, two women of about the same age, surrounded by velvet: couches, cushions, and drapes.

We talked about Johnny's reading. Marcella understands Johnny's successes and his failures. She understands that he has extreme difficulty settling down for more than two to three minutes at a time. She just doesn't know what to do about it. She gestured with beautifully lacquered nails to illustrate her point and shook her jeweled hair. The light from the window caught on the beads embedded in her braids, sending bright darts against the walls of the room as she shrugged her shoulders. We laughed together. I felt my paleness, my lack of glamour, sitting across from her in the large white house on the corner of Parkland and Thirty-fifth Avenue.

I left some puzzles and word lists for her to do with him when she could. I think our combined efforts are making a difference; Johnny can now stay in his seat for ten minutes at a time. He has also, for the first time, asked to read a book on his own.

Mitchell eats the school breakfast regularly, which keeps him awake the entire first hour. He completed his first crossword puzzle the other day. Audrey, his mother, has stopped in once more and calls me weekly.

These are the ones who stay.

There are other students, the ones I think of as the nomads. They come to school for a month or two and then disappear, to the reservation, to jail, to the streets. They reappear weeks later, get out their folders, and begin work again as though they hadn't been gone at all. I never quite adjust to their departures or to their returns.

Anthony is one of them. When he appears for class with his long, fur-collared coat, felt hat, and gold-topped cane, it is clear that he is trying hard to be a pimp. He looks ridiculous in the midst of ninth-grade girls with tiny legs and a thousand braids. Last June, during summer school, he waited for me every morning on the steps of the building, dressed for the heat in shorts and a T-shirt, drinking Coke, and eating a hot dog at 8 A.M. He wanted to learn to read, so I told him I'd work with him before school began.

"Need to be greasin'," he'd say, holding up his food, "then I'll come in with you."

We'd have a quiet half hour, I with my coffee, he with the second half of his can of pop. We'd sit together and work, the sweat collecting around his neck, his shirt already sticking to his back. This was the best time of day for Anthony. He was calm then. He seemed to start each morning over and so, in the earliest hours, he was fresh, held no grudges, was able to concentrate on the task in front of him. He'd struggle with vowels, trying to make the connection between their small sounds and the words he knew.

The court had assigned Anthony to a group home in Minneapolis last spring after he was caught in his second burglary attempt. Before this living arrangement at the home, he had come to school right off the streets, his coat heavy with dirt and grease, his shoes scuffed and filled with holes, stuffed with newspaper. He had come and curled in the corner of the room, dozing off, smelling of his slept-in clothes, cigarette smoke, and stale food. When startled awake, he became angry, showed his fists. But then, at the home, under the supervision of tough, loving, African American men and women, Anthony began to work hard, to come to school in clean clothes, wide awake. Under court order there, and under curfew, he seemed to flourish.

We told his probation officer that after his six-month stay at the home was over, he needed to be reassigned there: we had seen a transformation, but we didn't believe it would last without this kind of reinforcement for some more time. However, there was a waiting list for the already crowded home. Anthony had met all the conditions of the probation and he was allowed to leave.

And now, this fall, he is beginning to drift away again. When he comes to class he is dressed in silver and fur. He drops in only now and then to pay his respects, to tip his large felt hat, to take off his fur coat and drape it over the back of the chair. When he takes off that coat, he takes off his shoulders. For a few minutes, bent over a book, he looks and sounds like the Anthony of the summer, with his necklace of sweat, his voice repeating syllables over and over in the morning heat.

I must remember that no matter what we say or what we do, or what others do, some of these kids will be here in school for only a few months. They will work next to me, our heads bent together over a book. Then they will disappear. I might see one of them from my car window, hands in the pockets of deep coats, collar turned up against the winter evening.

They live off the streets, panhandling, dealing, moving across downtown with a purpose. When they sit in classrooms, they look like any other kids. They add columns in math classes, pick out the adjectives in English class. Almost miraculously they manage to find places to take showers, to get clothes, to come to school on the bus nearest the place where they have been sleeping the night before. Only their sudden disappearances make them different. When they are gone, they stand out, become noticeable.

Today, November 3rd, Anthony has decided to join us during first hour, flaunting his cane. He is dressed in a shiny suit and a large green hat. Sandy is in class as usual, and she is in a bad mood. She has just returned from Chicago, where, apparently, she was badly disappointed. Rhonda told me last week that Sandy has become obsessed with meeting the father she has never known, just to learn who he is, what he looks like. She found an uncle on this trip, but neither he nor his friends knew where Sandy's father had gone. Her dad had been in some kind of minor trouble and left town a few years ago. Sandy slumps in her seat, her wool coat tight around her shoulders.

Anthony, sensing her mood, snipes at her. Johnny joins in, getting her back for all the times she's teased him about his height. I am trying to keep them all occupied at their own desks, finding worksheets and word puzzles for them.

Rarely do I get desperate enough to use candy, but this is one of those days. With the promise of Snickers bars at the end of the hour, they settle down, a response that always surprises me. Many of these kids work part time after school. They can afford their own candy bars, big ones, not the miniatures I offer. Yet as soon as I promise them Snickers, they pull work out of their folders and become silent, concentrating. We make an exchange: their silence for my chocolate. They accept that there are times to bargain.

Peace is not to last. I hear a loud, female voice yelling from the end of the hall.

"I never wanted to come to this fuckin' school, and I'm not goin to stay in this cocksuckin' school. No one can make me stay no matter what you fuckers try to do!"

These words carry perfectly, high-pitched, getting closer. The coordinator's low voice can be heard after each outburst.

Anthony smiles. "Ol' Jackie comin' to this school." He shakes his head.

"Things'll get jumpin' around here now, Landsman."

"You know her?" I ask. Anthony and Johnny nod and laugh. Jackie's voice has lowered slightly, but we can still hear her words.

"I been away from my mama for a long time, fucker, so don't tell me what my mama says."

Johnny shakes his head.

"She's trouble, Landsman. I know that!"

He and Anthony slap palms.

Sandy slumps down in her seat.

The door to my classroom opens. Ted Marvin moves Jackie into the room.

"Mrs. Landsman, Jackie Simmons is here. She'll be in your first hour."

Jackie wears high heels and long yellow silk pants. The yellow top to her outfit is flimsy, falling off one shoulder. Her white skin looks like a baby's, and her hair is straight and clean, cascading down over one side of her face, pulled back behind her ear on the other side. She has long rhinestone earrings that rest against her neck. She looks Scandinavian with her blond hair and prominent cheekbones.

"Fuck these bums," she says, catching sight of Anthony. She stands with one hand on her hip.

"What's this little one doin' here?" She points to Johnny and smiles. He smiles back.

Sandy pulls her body up straight, opens a book, and turns away from the others. Jackie notices this but decides not to comment. She turns to Davey.

"Saw you and your little porno friend in the park," she says, matter-of-factly.

Davey looks at her with his blue eyes, and I suddenly notice how curly the lashes are, how perfectly pink his cheeks. I am frightened for him and for his friend Karen, the skinny child who smokes continuously and is one of the nomads. She hasn't stopped by my door in days. Davey shrugs, looks down at his book, refuses to connect with my eyes.

"Shut your fuckin' mouth," Anthony yells, angry.

Jackie's voice gathers volume, "You don't tell me nothin', pimp man. You don't tell me when to talk and when not to talk. I know my rights. I got free speech."

Anthony stands.

I jump up, walk over to Jackie, and say to the class, "I'd like to talk with Jackie for a few minutes alone. You guys keep working. See if you can earn the Snickers bars."

"What Snickers bars?" asks Jackie, attentive, her eyes fixed on me for the first time.

"Oh, I've promised them a candy bar if they can get through the hour. It's been a tough morning."

"Baby shit, candy," she says, but quietly, under her breath.

Anthony stares at us, then sits down, draping his coat over his shoulders like a cape. He sets his hat on his head at an angle.

I place a chair next to mine and motion to it. Jackie sits down, takes out a stick of gum, and puts it in her mouth. I ask her to read some words for me. She whips through them easily. I ask her what she likes to read about, what kind of books she'd like to work in.

She cracks her gum. "Books about dogs. I never had no dog," she says.

"Okay. We'll find something about dogs. For now, why don't you try this worksheet?" For a moment fear shadows her face. Then she looks at the worksheet, sees that it is easy, and takes it over to an empty chair between Johnny and Mitchell. For the first time in a month, Mitchell has put his head down on the desk.

Jackie pushes at him. He keeps his head down but tells her to stop. She leans over and whispers in his ear. She rests her body next to his. He edges away from her in his chair, keeping his head down the entire time.

"He can't have any Snickers bar, can he?" asks Davey.

"Not if he doesn't get to work," I answer.

"Aw, shit, Landsman," Mitchell says, looking up. "How we s' posed to work when bigmouth here is talking in our ears?"

"You were already not workin' when I talked in your ear!" says Jackie.

"He was jus' tryin' to keep from lookin' at you!" puts in Sandy.

"What you sayin', girl?" Jackie gets up.

"Don't bother me none," says Sandy, and she stands up to face Jackie.

I walk between them as the bell rings.

"That's it. Go to your next class."

Jackie and Sandy stare each other down.

"Hey, Landsman, where's my Snickers bar?" asks Johnny.

I begin handing out candy, knowing that Sandy won't be able to resist. She moves away from Jackie and over to me. She holds out her hand.

"Candy is baby shit," says Jackie. With that she turns on her high heels and walks out of my room.

Sandy follows her, at a distance.

Anthony waits until the others have gone before quietly holding out his hand. I drop a Snickers bar into it. He smiles, pulls his coat around his body with a sweeping gesture, and walks out of the room.

I sink back in my chair but almost immediately one of the quiet boys from second hour comes in and sits down next to me.

"I know what I want to be now. I know what I want to do when I get older."

"What's that, Ben?"

"I want to be a weather dermatologist!"

I hold onto my laughter.

"Not dermatologist, Ben. You want to be a meteorologist. That's someone who predicts the weather. You warn people about tornadoes and snowstorms."

"Yeah," he answers. "That's it."

The rest of the day goes smoothly. I try not to think of Jackie as I ride home in the afternoon. The whole mood of a class changes when a new student comes into it. This change will be more difficult than most.

Jackie knows the kids' secrets. She knows what they do at night, how each of them spends his time. She recognizes Johnny and calls Anthony a pimp. She is unnerving because she is one of those people who says what most of us would rather not hear. I wonder what she'll sense about me.

When I get home after a meeting downtown, I want good food: carrots shredded next to pale zucchini, rice, chicken, and ice cream. The kitchen seems to be the only place I can relax. Maury is already there, beginning to make an early supper. He takes off his glasses, leans over the wok, his back curved over it. I tell him: "Linda is not sleeping now." I say: "Johnny is trying to find a job, but no one believes he is sixteen." The meat sizzles when Maury drops it into the oil. "And I have a new student named Jackie." Maury listens with his body.

Later, when we make love, I think: this is what I need, and this and this. I think: Davey looked tired this morning, the streets are getting colder, and Frankie has no socks.

The next day, Jackie doesn't make it to to my class. She apparently argued with another young woman on the bus and when they arrived at school the two began pulling at each other's hair, rolling on the floor in front of the entryway. I didn't see any of this, just heard the story from the principal. Both girls are suspended for three days.

In the lounge, over lunch, we talk about Jackie. None of us are surprised at her behavior, remembering the conference we had about her. Yet we also remember a translucence, a vulnerability about her.

"She's trouble," says Mary, shaking her head, echoing the kids. "She's trouble, and she's smart."

"I kind of like her," I say. "I know she's set off all the kids in my class, but I like her."

"You're crazy, girl," Mary says, smiling, shaking her head. I know she likes Jackie.

"Where's she living now?" I ask. "Anyone know?"

Jill, the home ec teacher and Jackie's "case manager," looks up from her salad. Jill always brings the most elegant salads, sealed in Tupperware. Today she has tiny shrimp and pale lettuce and deep red and yellow peppers.

"She's supposed to be at home, but her mother says she's only there three nights a week at the most."

Mary shakes her head again. We change the topic, talk about the Vikings, their chances for the play-offs, the skill of Fran Tarkington and Chuck Foreman. We talk about Christmas and its craziness, the fact that decorations are already up. Twenty-two minutes later, the lunch bell rings and we busy ourselves cleaning up, throwing away bags, brushing crumbs off the table. Jill takes a last drag on her cigarette, Mary gets up slowly, pulling her sweater around her large shoulders.

"When will Jackie come back?" I ask.

"They'll count today, Tuesday, so that means—today, Wednesday, and Thursday she's out. Friday, then. But she doesn't like to come to school on Fridays."

"Probably Monday," I say, picking up my grade book and my unread mail. Jill nods as we part, each heading toward class.

When Jackie returns to school the following Monday, she is dressed in a short coat with a fur collar and tight pants made of a flimsy material, despite the cold weather. She insists on high heels, even on the slick streets, and goes without a hat. Her lips are blue from the cold; she has been smoking outside the building door. The kids sense that my attention has shifted to Jackie, and they resent it. They revert to old behaviors. Sandy sulks, refusing to take off her coat. Mitchell sleeps away the last ten minutes of class, and Johnny jumps around the room the way he did in September, talking about his height again. Anthony drops in and out; Davey becomes sullen, turns his whole body away from me when I approach his seat. Outside, the gray chill of November falls in wet rain, bringing down the last of the brown leaves.

About two weeks later, one dark morning before first hour, as Sandy sits in her usual place across from me, I notice her deep frown and feel a hostility coming from her that is almost uncontainable. It builds as we sit together. She makes a wall of books between us, taking them from the shelves and piling them up until I cannot see her head.

"Hey!" I call out. "Where the hell are you?"

"None of your business, Landsman, and you're not suppose to say 'hell.' " Her voice is tight.

"Yeah, it's my business, Sandy."

"No, it ain't. It's my business."

I don't say anything. We could go on arguing about whose business it is all morning.

I get up and walk around her fortress. She sits, staring straight ahead. I put my hand on her shoulder. I have touched Sandy only a few times. I can usually sense which students need and want touch and which are almost phobic, cannot be approached. Today she whirls around and swings one arm out toward my hand. She knocks over the pile of books. I pull away from her.

"Leave me alone, Landsman." She begins piling up the books again to close herself in.

"You got some work to do?" I ask. "Your folder in there?"

"Yeah. That all you care about, work to do?"

"No. That's not all," I say. "I care about you, about why you're so angry today."

"No, you don't care about that," she says.

Jackie comes in with Johnny and Mitchell following her.

"Please, just one!" Johnny whines, pulling on Jackie's arm.

"No, man, I need 'em."

"Give 'im one so's he'll shut up," says Mitchell, smiling.

Jackie shrugs. Johnny moves around behind her, toward her pocket. She pushes him away gently.

"Aw, come on, man, just one."

Jackie smiles. She reaches in her coat and pulls out a Snickers bar of her own. She waves it in front of Johnny. He dances back and forth in front of her as she moves the candy. Mitchell shakes his head. Sandy adds more books to her pile.

I walk over to them.

"Okay. Put it away if you're not going to share it. You're just teasing him."

"They like to be teased," she says, laughing. "Guys like to be teased, don't they, little Johnny?"

Johnny is acting his height. He whines again.

"Come on, Jackie, just a half of one."

I reach out and snatch the candy bar. Immediately, I realize I have done the wrong thing. Sandy applauds from behind her books. Before I can stop her, Jackie whirls out of her chair and knocks the books toward Sandy's head. They fall all over the table.

Sandy jumps up.

This time I put my body between them.

"Why you let her do that?" Sandy says, glaring at me.

"I couldn't stop her in time," I say.

"Why you take *my* candy?" yells Jackie. She rests her hands on her hips. "I don't take *your* candy!"

"That candy was causing too much trouble," I say. Meanwhile Johnny has slumped down in his chair and Mitchell has, of course, put his head on the table. Davey stands in the doorway, taking in the scene.

"What's going on?" he asks.

"Nothin'," says Johnny.

"Fuck, it's nothin'!" snarls Davey, sitting down next to Mitchell.

Sandy retreats behind her books. She doesn't open her folder, but sits stony-eyed and perfectly still.

I ask Jackie and Johnny to come out into the hall.

"We need to settle this now," I say.

"She bein' mean," says Johnny. He puts his thumb in his mouth, something he hasn't done since last year. It seems so incongruous to see him dressed in his tie and baggy pants, sucking on his thumb.

"Ain't he cute, Landsman?" Jackie winks at me.

"Yeah, real cute," I say, sarcastically. He takes his thumb out of his mouth.

"Everything different when she comes," says Johnny. "Even you different, Landsman. Shit!" He kicks the locker near him.

"Here, baby, here's some fuckin' candy!" Jackie takes another Snickers bar out of her pants pocket and throws it at Johnny. He puts his hand up to keep it from hitting his face. The candy falls on the tiled floor and Johnny quickly bends to pick it up.

"Okay, now," I say. "Can you two come back in and get to work?"

"Yeah," says Johnny.

Jackie doesn't say anything. She rolls her eyes and stares at the back of a young man who is collecting attendance sheets.

"I can't let you back in unless you think you can handle being there," I say. Jackie refuses to speak. I am stuck. I was sure she'd be able to promise to work. I tell Johnny to get back to the room and start his next worksheet and tell Jackie to come with me to the office. She follows reluctantly. I take her into Ted Marvin's office. He looks up from his desk, surprised to see me.

"She needs to sit this class out," I say.

"You need to sit your life out!" Jackie yells.

Ted nods his head toward a chair. Jackie sits down.

"I've got to get back to my class," I say. "Can we meet later?"

"Yes," he says. "Come in at the end of the hour."

I walk back into my room, feeling utterly defeated. The kids cheer when they see that Jackie isn't with me. Sandy takes down her fortress. Davey smiles his genuine smile. They work the rest of the hour, harder than I've ever seen them work.

Later, in Ted Marvin's office, Jackie still sits in the same chair, chewing gum. I give her the fur jacket she left in my room, the pockets bulging with more candy bars and chewing gum.

Ted asks me what commitment I need from Jackie in order for her to return to my class.

"I need her to stop teasing the kids. She could really be a help in there. Right now, she's got them upset."

"You're the one who gets them upset!" Jackie glares at me.

"I don't wave Snickers bars in their faces. I don't push over their books." My voice has risen. I find myself arguing with Jackie. I have lost control.

Ted jumps in.

"What do you need to be able to make it in Mrs. Landsman's room?" he asks Jackie.

"Nothin'." She looks at the floor.

"Can you go in there tomorrow and work?"

"Yeah." She cracks her gum. Her hair covers her face. She slumps in her seat.

"Good," I say. "I wonder if you'd listen to Johnny read once in a while. He needs some extra help."

"You help him, that's your job." She looks at me defiantly.

"Right," I answer, looking back at her, evenly. "I just thought you'd be able to help out."

"Yeah, sure, anything you say." She gets up from the chair. She stands in front of Ted, hand on hip.

"Tomorrow, then," he says and waves us both away. Jackie walks quickly into the hallway. She never looks back at me.

Later, in the lounge, I describe the whole scene. No one tells me that I blew it or that I handled it well. They're sympathetic, because, especially in this program, some days are like this.

"I thought you liked her," says Bart, the math teacher, a twinkle in his eye.

"I do. I still do. I don't know why, either, except that she's got that fight in her."

"Yeah. Just great," Bart says. "Exactly what we need. Someone else with some fight in them."

"You want to come out to her mom's with me this afternoon? I'm making a home visit," says Jill.

"Okay."

"We'll take separate cars. I've got to be home by 4:15 or so."

Later that day we drive to Mrs. Simmons' small brick house tucked into the middle of a neat block of small brick houses. Jackie's mother stands in her entryway, next to a pile of men's and women's boots and army fatigue overcoats. Unlike Marcella Washington, Mrs. Simmons does not offer us coffee. She does not invite us to sit down on the floral-printed, old New England-style couch. She does not lead us out of the draft from the doorway. We three stand in the entrance, surrounded by wool caps and umbrellas.

"She's been gone two days. Haven't seen her since the night before her suspension was over. Just took off. Don't even know where to look."

"She was in school today," I say. "She had a rough time in my room."

"Yeah. That's Jackie. She has a rough time everywhere she goes." Mrs. Simmons smiles fleetingly, and I detect in that smile affection, but affection that has fled and cannot be revived right now.

"The cops have brought her back here a couple of times. But I can't seem to keep her. She'll sneak out windows to get away."

"She comes back sometimes," says Jill, looking toward the living room. Jill is tired from being on her feet all day and would like to be asked to sit down. Mrs. Simmons holds her position.

"Yeah. She keeps tryin' it. Then we fight. Then she leaves." Mrs. Simmons chews her gum loudly in the silence that follows.

"She seems to want to go to school, though. She keeps trying that," I say.

"Oh. Yeah. She used to love school. She was so good when she was little."

"She's a good reader," I say, inanely searching for a way to keep this woman talking.

"She ain't never had no trouble readin'," says Mrs. Simmons. "Used to get lots of stars for her readin'."

Again I detect something in the memory, some softening in Mrs. Simmons' voice, in her throat. Even her eyes lose their careful look for just a moment.

"Well. I wish there was something we could do," says Jill, turning toward the door. "Is there anything?"

"Just send her home if she shows up. Tell her to come on home and stay," says Mrs. Simmons, shrugging her shoulders again. And in a defeated reversal of purpose—we had gone to see whether Jackie's mother could help us work with Jackie—we leave, promising to help Mrs. Simmons reunite with her daughter if we can.

The wind has quieted. The sky is darkening already and the trees are bare, sculpted dark branches against the grayness. Jill unlocks her car door, starts the engine, and rolls down her window.

"I don't like this. I hate it when the kids fall through the cracks like this."

"I know."

"I'll tell Jane. Maybe they can find Jackie a place to live somewhere else."

"Yeah. Let's send her to Jane—when she comes in." We nod, relieved, partly because we have found a verbal solution, partly because the solution involves sending Jackie to someone else who may be able to help.

As I unlock my car, I see Jackie walking quickly up the street. She is shivering, her legs bare in high heels.

"What you doin' here?" she asks.

"Mrs. Clancy and I just finished making a home visit," I say, trying to sound casual.

"Oh." She takes a drag on her cigarette, then drops it on the ground and grinds it out.

"My ma don't like cigarettes in her house," she says and turns away from me to walk up her front path.

The next morning Jackie comes up to my desk. Sandy is already barricaded behind her books. Johnny is reading and Davey is resting his head on his hand.

"Can I work with Mitchell instead of Johnny?" Jackie whispers.

"Sure," I say. "Let's wait a few minutes until everyone gets settled down."

Once the bell has rung and Mitchell opens his folder, Jackie settles next to him.

"You get me," she says. He looks over at her and smiles. She takes off her coat and her sweater. She is wearing a T-shirt that says "Not for Sale" on it. Today the room is stifling. Yesterday we froze.

I show Jackie Mitchell's flash cards and leave the two of them together. Sandy is watching them intently, mouthing the syllables as Mitchell says them. Jackie is mouthing them, too. Their faces are concentrating on the flash card Jackie holds in her ringed fingers. I should have thought of this tactic yesterday, first thing.

This afternoon Mr. Lee visits my room after school is over for the day. His son, Frankie, the one with the clean clothes, the one who told me about eating 'coon, is a nomad returned. They have been in Mississippi for a month. Mr. Lee puts his hat in his hand as he comes toward my desk.

"I'm Frankie's father. That man in the suit out there said you're Frankie's readin' teacher."

"Yes, I am. How do you do, Mr. Lee?" I stand up, hold out my hand. He sways a little as he sits down across from my desk.

"I want Frankie to be readin'," he says, his hat in his lap.

"Frankie can learn very well if he can keep coming to school," I say.

Mr. Lee smiles, showing that he has only two top front teeth. His eyes are yellow filmed. The kids say that he has been in prison. I show him Frankie's folder and go over the lists of words Frankie is working on, as well as the flash cards and the worksheets. Frankie is fourteen years old, reading at first-grade level.

Mr. Lee bends over the flash cards, intent on each sound. He asks me to explain to him how they work, what the sounds are, so he can help Frankie. I explain that his son is trying to read twenty-five cards in twenty-five seconds. I tell him it is important that Frankie learn the sounds so well that he will hear them automatically when he reads. Then I show him the lists of words that have those sounds as part of them.

"Frankie read all these?" he asks.

"Most of them," I answer. "He's working on speed now."

"Maybe I can take a set and practice these with him, so he gets them faster."

I give him an extra set of cards, more word sheets and worksheets. I also find an extra copy of the book Frankie is reading.

"Good luck," I say and smile.

He puts his dark hand around the folder full of words. He nods his head. "I'll help Frankie get through these."

"When you think he's ready for the next set at home, you come in and let me know. If you need more help with Frankie, there are some night classes in reading here."

"Yes. Well, thank you now," he says as he gets up. He walks out of the room more firmly than he came in. After he leaves I sit and wonder whether he knew that I knew he was the one who wanted to learn to read, and that these materials were really for him. I hope not. I hope he returns for more materials for his son.

The days move along easily for a few weeks. Jackie helps Mitchell struggle through his words, sounding out each letter with him, her mouth agonizing like his mouth as he tries every letter one at a time until he can hear it in his head. She is the only person he'll work with besides me. Sandy's fortress is lower each day until she has a circle around her only two books high. Davey stands at the window at the end of the hour, talking to Jackie. Once in awhile she ruffles his blond hair. Once she even put her arm around his shoulders. Johnny sits quietly for twenty minutes at a time.

One day Jackie comes in smelling of a sweetness I can't quite name: a combination of marijuana, sex, and perfume. I know she's been on the streets. Her mother says she's rarely home. The kids say she's got a pimp now.

Jackie says she wants to work alone this morning. She stares out the window all hour. Sandy takes down the last of her barricade of books. Davey smiles at Jackie with a new kindness in his eyes. Johnny, for the first time in a year, is silent. Five minutes before the final bell Jackie asks for a pass to the social worker. I fill it out for her and walk her to the door. Impulsively, I call out, "Good luck," as she walks down the hall. She nods her head but doesn't turn around.

Maybe it is the silence in the corridor that reminds me of a distance in my own childhood that was never crossed. Watching Jackie move away, I remember the hallway in the house where I grew up, the beautiful tweed carpet on the floor, the lemon smell on the antique wood, the bay window filled with cut glass. I feel a loneliness, thinking about those rooms, that entryway, a baby grand piano under the sunny window in the music room. As Jackie turns the corner, some emotion makes her body in black leather pants seem unbearably vulnerable.

Later, Jane tells me that she thinks she can get Jackie into a program for teen prostitutes and runaways. There's a waiting list, but she has some hope and she will exert whatever pull she has.

Always the lists, the endless names of the kids who are waiting for help.

A week later another nomad, Carol Makepeace, reappears. Carol is Native American, back from the reservation. We have always gotten along well, and I am pleased to see her again. She tells me she has run away from the hospital two days after being hit by a car. She has landed on the streets with no money. Her elbow rests at an odd angle, a geometry I can't understand until she tells me that she has cut away her cast.

Carol is a voracious reader and heads immediately to the shelf for a book. She stops when she sees Jackie's head bent next to Mitchell's.

"Hey, girl. You here now?" she asks.

Jackie looks up, and Mitchell does, too.

"Yeah, girl. I go here." Jackie smiles, as pleased to see Carol as Carol is to see her. I had no idea they knew each other, yet I'm not surprised. There is a network, a community of street kids who drift in and out of each others' lives just the way they drift in and out of mine.

"You shouldn't've cut away that ol' cast, girl. Your arm gonna hang there funny all the time now," says Jackie.

"I hate them doctors," says Carol quietly.

"Don't matter. You shouldn't mess up your arm like that."

Jackie pushes her hair back from her face and curls it behind one ear. The sun rests on her white skin, bringing up a flush, a delicate pink under her paleness.

"You shouldn't hang around on Hennepin Avenue, neither," says Johnny.

"I just visit," Jackie says, looking over at me quickly. "Got lots of friends on the street."

"Oh, yeah, just visitin'," says Johnny. "Sure, girl."

"Shut up, little guy," says Jackie, but she's smiling. "I'm gonna be in a group home. Movin' in next week."

She pushes Mitchell gently. He rests his cheek on one arm and looks up at her.

"You do what you do," Carol says, shrugging. "Remember last spring, I saw you out on the streets then, too."

"Yeah. You can't stay with your mom, you find your own place," says Jackie.

Davey looks up. "Yeah," he says, barely animated. "You find your own place." Instead of teasing him, Jackie looks at him hard.

"Some places kind of dangerous," she says.

"So?" says Davey. He turns back to the window, hunches up his shoulders, and stares outside. Carol picks at the places on the skin of her arm where the adhesive held the cast.

Sandy has not bothered to turn away. She keeps her body upright, listening.

Jackie looks at her. "You stay with your mom?" she asks Sandy.

"My mom's dead."

"That's cold," says Jackie.

"I stay with my aunt," Sandy says.

"Wish I had a aunt. My mom kicks me out, and I don't got no aunt," says Jackie.

"That when you slept by the lake?" asks Mitchell.

"Yeah. 'Til it got too cold. Then I stayed over at my friends'. Then their parents found out."

I try to imagine the different places Jackie has hidden, the basements, the old cars, the entryways to condemned buildings. In the summers the park police would make her move on in the morning.

"Then where'd you go?" asks Johnny.

"Then, you know, my friend put me up," she looks at Carol, who shrugs and repeats, "You do what you gotta do."

Johnny carefully adjusts his shirt cuffs until their pale yellow protrudes evenly from his beige sweater.

"Yeah. Well," Jackie says hesitantly, "I needed cigarettes and some clothes, man. I didn't have nothin'." She shivers. No one speaks. None of them seem surprised at Jackie's story. Sandy doesn't say a word: no reprimand, no religious warning.

I drive home that evening thinking about Carol and Jackie at fifteen. At their age I was in a boarding school in New England. Swans glided by in the pond outside my window. The sound of the ball hitting the field-hockey stick echoed over the manicured lawns of St. Margaret's. I wouldn't have thought of running away. I stayed for every after-supper hymn, for every good-night bell. There was nothing of the Carol Makepeace in me: I would not have hopped a bus for North Dakota to sit on the front steps of an uncle's shack. I waited at the window on Sundays after church, watching for my gentleman "visitor." I would not have stood, as Jackie had, at a corner on Saturday nights, waiting for the first car to glide by and pull up to the curb.

Two days later Jane tells me that Jackie has officially moved into the group home.

By mid-November all the kids in our entire program have earned 300 points for a field trip. The fifty-four students reach consensus on a trip to a bowling alley as their reward. These outings are always risky ventures. Away from the restraint of school the kids may behave like angels—or disappear, deal drugs, taunt passersby. A majority of the teachers in the program accompany them.

This time, although they seem pumped up, they do not make faces or hold obscene signs out of the back of the bus as we head off. They do not give the finger to the drivers in cars behind the bus. We arrive peacefully, the kids tumbling out and into the alley, lining up for shoes, setting up groups at the various stations.

We have rented four sections of the alley. The retired men's group at the other end of the wide, lighted room moves into an impromptu huddle. They sneak glances our way, gauge the number of adults (eight) to the number of kids, and relax a little, going back to bowling, smoking, and talking quietly.

All of our students bowl today, even the ones who have never tried it before. Sandy stands too straight, can't seem to bend her body low enough, so her first ball bounces hard on the lane and dribbles off to the side. Johnny runs up and shows her how, stooping over and letting his arm follow through. She doesn't smile but concentrates hard, lowering her body by bending her knees just the way he showed her. The ball rolls slowly down the center of the lane; when it reaches the pins it barely pushes four of them over. Sandy turns toward the scoring table with a wide smile on her face. She even gives Johnny the high-five slap before she sits down. Her skirt is loose today, allowing her to move a little more easily than the narrow ones she has been wearing.

Johnny bowls well. His only problems are concentration and patience. Once in a while the ball goes wild, shoots off to the side and into the alley next to his. He has difficulty waiting his turn, too, hopping from alley to alley, talking animatedly to the older gentlemen at the other end of the room.

Mitchell is the best bowler of all. He has surprising strength in his thin arms. He takes his time, squints down the lane, and lays the ball out smoothly. He gets three strikes before the game is over.

Jackie appears indifferent, yet she also seems more relaxed than I've seen her. Today she has on a clean T-shirt and jeans, her hair pulled back into a long barrette that rests on the nape of her neck. When it is her turn, she puts down her Coke, grabs the nearest ball, takes aim, and lets go. She doesn't look at the result of her throw but turns toward the rack and selects her next ball. As soon as the pin setter is removed she fires, then immediately sits down, squinting from her seat to see the number of pins left. She occasionally ruffles Davey's blond hair or passes the Coke to Johnny when he hops by on his way to the vending machine for candy.

Linda keeps score. She doesn't want to bowl, but the kids convince her to try. She bowls slowly and weakly, hurrying back behind the desk after the second ball has left her hand. Once she gets an eight and the others clap. Frankie has never bowled before but no one helps him as he stands, hesitant, his bare feet in bowling shoes that are too big. I know I cannot give him instruction; he would lose face. Bill, one of the male teachers along on the trip, comes over and shows Frankie how to stand, and on his second ball, all the pins go down, one by one. Linda claps and Mitchell shakes his head in disbelief. Johnny jumps up for his turn, saying back over his shoulder, "That ain't nothin', man. Watch this." He lets the ball fly. It curves off sharply into the gutter. Sandy chuckles and looks slyly at me. At the slight shake of my head, she stops laughing. For his second ball, Johnny stands quietly at the end of the lane, takes careful aim and lets it go down the middle. He gets an eight and struts back to a seat, his pressed blue jeans and shirt unwrinkled and perfect, smooth against his small body.

Frankie is smiling a wide, sweet smile that hasn't left his face since he made the strike. He sits two seats from Linda, shivering slightly. I offer him some peanuts and a drink from my Coke. When he gets up again, he bowls a two on the first ball and a four on the second. He moves next to Linda, watching her keep score. She explains to him exactly what she is doing, and he stays at her side the remainder of the two hours we are at the alley.

Anthony never bowls, choosing instead to stroll the restaurant in his fur coat and hat, holding his cane.

When we round up the students for the bus ride home, I notice restlessness and muted anger as they stand in line, waiting to turn in their shoes. I hear some sniping, some comments from the guys about young women in the group. I see a few of the newer male students nudging each other, pointing at

Jackie and Linda. Students I don't know very well jab at each other then dance away.

On the ride back I take a seat near the middle of the bus with Mary next to me; two other teachers sit in the back and three nearer the front for the half-hour drive to school. A young man named Martin moves up to the vacant seat next to Linda. He begins pulling at her hair. I ask Martin to stop, to move back to his original seat. He moves one seat behind Linda and rests his hand on the back of her seat, right behind her neck. His friend Joseph, new to the program this week, whispers to him. Martin laughs and once again begins to play with Linda's hair. Linda ducks her head but doesn't turn. Meanwhile, three boys move a seat behind where Mindy, another new student in the program, sits with Carol Makepeace. The boys suddenly blow up balloons they have kept in their pockets and tie them in knots. Standing up and holding them in front of their bodies like giant phalluses, they push them at the girls. We teachers stand up and order them to move. Bill and I slide into seats next to them. Other boys begin taunting more of the girls, whispering in their ears. Linda curls into the corner of her seat, leaning away from Joseph's breath as he reaches for her. I have no choice but to keep my seat next to one of the boys who still has a balloon in his hand and is masturbating it, grinning at a girl who sighs, shakes her head, and turns away.

Suddenly Jackie's voice can be heard above the others, just the way we heard it weeks ago when she arrived for classes.

"Get your fuckin' hands off me, boy, or I'll hit you so's you can't use your real pecker no more." I look back. Jackie is leaning over her seat glaring at a young man who was obviously rolling a balloon against her back. He sits down and stares sullenly out the window.

"I'm warnin' you," I hear from up front. "You come near me and I'll hit you upside your head." This statement comes from Sandy, her voice quieter, deeper than usual. Anthony frowns at her, then moves to another seat. Carol leans back over the seat she is sharing with Mindy. She uses her good arm to smack Trent in the face. Mindy shrinks down in her seat.

By the time we arrive at school, buses are waiting to take the students home. As they get off the field-trip bus, we tell them we will meet with them in the morning to talk about their behavior. All of the staff assemble in the conference room for a "war council." I am stunned. I am angry. I am not sure how to define some other feeling that sits on my shoulders, causing me to curve inward, to slouch, the posture my father taught me never to assume. We decide to suspend the worst offenders for two days and to provide in-school, all-day detention for the others.

Mary speaks up, finally, saying, "Some of those new girls, those quiet ones, don't know how to keep these men away. We got to do something for them."

"I mean, some of our girls can take care of business just fine," she says. "But the others need some street sense."

"The young men need some damn control, some manners," says Bill, followed by nods of assent from the rest of us.

"We'll deal with that first thing in the morning in group. We'll have group at the beginning of the day and go on as long as it takes," says Ted Marvin.

"But what about those girls?" insists Mary. "They need somethin', honey. Jackie took those boys on! She could show the rest of them a thing or two."

After the meeting we are all exhausted.

Mary says to me, "You look pretty down, girl."

"I am," I say, my voice trembling a little. "I am."

"Well, let's do something then," says Mary. "We could get these girls together and have a women's class. You know about that kind of stuff."

"Maybe," I say, weighted with the idea.

"You could do it, girl. You know all about that feminism. And I could come sometimes."

"I don't know. I like the idea, but the whole thing feels so damn heavy for me."

Mary touches my arm. "It's okay, Julie. The kids can help each other. That Jackie can run the class for you." She chuckles. "Why, Joseph looked like he wanted to shrink up and disappear. Oooooh! She took him on with that mouth. Some of these other girls need a little of that mouth."

"See you, Mary," I say, heading for my room.

"Think about it," she says.

Driving home, I know she is right. These girls do need each other. I just don't know if I should be the one helping them. It is dark already, a light snow falling. Maury has taken Aaron to his guitar lesson and afterwards they are going to eat dinner out, just the boys. I fix my usual yellow meal: applesauce, eggs, and toast. Even Mozart doesn't comfort me so I find an old Billie Holiday rerelease. Billie helps.

When Ted Marvin calls me later that evening to ask me to start a young women's group, I tell him that I'll try it. Ted confesses that he and Mary talked over the idea after I left and that she would be willing to help sometimes if I would like her to.

"I'd like," I say and hang up.

The next day I set up the group. It will include Sandy, Jackie, Carol, Linda, Mindy, and Davey's friend Karen. Mary adds a few more names. I plan field trips to a Teen Age Medical Center, discussions with ex-prostitutes, and birthday parties. I decide that this group won't avoid talking about sex, that it won't stay too sweet. As I plan over the next few weeks, I feel a different kind of tension than I've ever felt, a tension tight with the trip wire of memory, a tension that calls up one afternoon, a hot day and an eastern city from my past. I keep myself from remembering by being over-organized.

Snow flurries have started outside on this Wednesday afternoon before Thanksgiving. Friends have invited us over for a turkey dinner tomorrow, which means that Maury doesn't have to cook and I don't have to clean house. I have always preferred this long holiday weekend to the manic rush of Christmas. I am looking forward to leaving early to pick up some bread and salad ingredients on my way home. When Ted Marvin stops by my door I already have my coat on and am pulling out the desk drawer to get my purse.

"We need a late group tonight," he says. "The kids didn't deal with their problems in group today."

He notices my coat. "Sorry." He smiles.

I nod. He walks on to the next room.

Once every couple of months we hold "late group" for students who haven't been honest in the regular group sessions during the last hour of school. If they won't talk with each other about the kinds of behavior that got them into trouble that day, then the staff of our program holds an additional session and runs it.

Before the final bell, the teachers in the program and the two administrators make a circle of chairs in a classroom. Hall aides and group leaders escort five students down the hall. I can already hear Jackie: "Get your motherfuckin' hands off me, man. I'm goin' home. I got plans." Yet her voice is closer. She comes in first, stops a minute when she sees us, trying to decide whether to back out. An aide holds her gently, moves her toward a chair across from me and next to Jill. Jackie sits down and takes out a piece of gum. The other kids file in, scowling, and take their places in various seats around the room. The final bell rings. We can hear other students slamming their lockers, running down the hall, yelling to each other, glad to be out for the long weekend. The halls empty quickly. The secretary of our program is calling the parents who have phones to tell them that their kids will be late.

Johnny is the only other student from my classes who is part of the late group. He knows the score and says he'll go first.

Ted asks him to describe what problems he had that day. Apparently he hadn't mentioned in the regular group session that he walked across the tables during lunch hour in the cafeteria.

Johnny starts by describing first hour:

"Well, I was okay in Landsman's room most of the time."

I move purposefully in my seat.

"Except when I called Davey a fag," says Johnny.

I nod.

"And in second hour I threw some magazines on the floor and walked on them." He looks at Burt, who teaches him math second hour.

"And what else did you do?" asks Burt.

"I skated around the room on the magazines."

"Right."

"And then third hour I skipped class and went to the store. And fourth hour I brought candy into Golden's room."

"And what happened because of the candy?" asks Linda Golden.

"Everyone wanted some, and no one would work all hour."

Ted Marvin sits impassively recording this recital in his log with the title LATE GROUP scrawled across the cover in large block letters.

"What happened at lunch?" asks Sam, another administrator in our program.

"I got up and walked all over everybody's food," says Johnny. He giggles.

"You think that's funny?" asks Ted.

"No, man, except it was such a gross lunch, I don't think nobody minded much." There are more smiles and snickers from the other kids in the room. I work to keep my expression serious.

"You got that right!" says Jackie. "That is just slop in there."

"The man in charge of the lunchroom seemed to mind quite a bit," Ted says.

"What happened fifth hour?" asks Jill, the home ec teacher.

"Well, I cut up Marcella's niece's dress."

"How long had Marcella been working on that dress for her niece?"

Johnny shrugs his shoulders.

"About three weeks, Johnny," says Jill.

"Did anything else happen today?" Ted asks Johnny.

Johnny is silent a moment. Then he looks up. "What you mean?"

"Did you do anything else besides go to the store third hour?"

Johnny looks down at his hands. He pulls at the pleats on his pants. "Yeah."

"What else, Johnny?"

"I got high."

Ted and Sam look around the room.

"Does anyone have any more questions they want to ask Johnny?"

Burt says, "You weren't high, though, when you ruined all the magazines in my room, were you, Johnny?"

"No, man, I just did that."

There is a long silence. The radiators hiss and the walls creak. Ted clears his throat and says, "All I heard about was the lunchroom episode. But it sounds like your whole day was a problem, Johnny."

Johnny nods his head and looks down at his knees.

"What do you want to commit to do after the vacation? What do you think you can do to control your behavior?"

"I be all right after vacation. It was mostly the dope I smoked."

"So, you think you can earn all your points in Mrs. Landsman's room?"

"In all my classes, man, for two whole weeks." Johnny says this in a loud voice, nodding his head vigorously.

"You're saying you can be perfect in all your classes for two weeks: get to them on time, work all hour, keep your mouth shut?"

The rest of the students become restless, turn in their seats. Jackie sighs and cracks her gum. She taps one high heel on the floor.

"Yeah."

Ted shakes his head. "I don't think so. I don't want you to set up some commitment you can't keep. How about earning all your points the first three hours of the day. See how that goes for a week. And absolutely no trouble in the lunchroom and no dope. That sound all right?"

"Yeah. That sound right. I can do it in all my classes, though, Mr. Marvin. It ain't no problem."

"You try that. See if you can. Your commitment is for those three classes plus lunch for one week."

"Okay, man. Can I go?'

"You can go." Ted hands Johnny a bus token and Johnny practically runs to the door. Then he stops, turns around, and says, "You have a good Thanksgiving," to everyone in the room.

Our faces remain impassive.

"Can I go next?" asks Jackie.

"Okay," Ted flips to a new page in the log. "What problems did you have today, Jackie?"

"Didn't have no problems, man. Don't know why I'm here."

Ted flips to a new page and calls on Trent to describe his day.

"Fuck, man! You said it was my turn. I gotta get the hell out of here!" Jackie is furious.

"Trent, what happened fourth hour?" asks Ted, ignoring Jackie.

Trent describes his day and makes a commitment to quit fighting in the halls between classes. Jackie turns her back on the group. Ted interviews the rest of the students and the meeting moves quickly. After the others have left the room, he turns back to Jackie.

"Okay, go ahead, what happened today, Jackie."

"Fuck, man, it's fuckin' three-thirty!" she says.

No one speaks. The room is quiet. Already the afternoon is beginning to darken outside. The snow is coming down thicker, faster. One hall aide breaks the silence by jokingly asking for light or dark turkey meat preferences. Mary says she wants cranberry sauce. I know that many of the other teachers are going out of town tonight. They are trying to hide their own restlessness.

"You ready, Jackie?" Ted's voice is not unkind.

"I fucked up in my math class." Jackie shakes back her hair, pushes her chin out.

"Could you be more specific?"

"I told Jeremy that he must have a small pecker."

"And then what happened?" asked Burt.

"And then Jeremy cried. And then I said that only boys with small peckers cry."

"And?" Burt leans forward in his chair. It has clearly not been his day, either.

"And then the class laughed, and then we all started throwing paper at Jeremy."

"And what happened when I asked you to leave?"

"I wouldn't go."

"What did you do?"

"I said I liked bein' in a room full of small peckers." Jackie smiles when she says this.

"Did anything else happen today?" asks Ted.

"In my class?" I ask.

"Naw. Not in your ol' dumb class."

There is silence again.

"Oh, yeah." Jackie shrugs her shoulders. "Yeah, well that wasn't nothin' big."

"What wasn't anything big?" asks Ted.

"Well, at the end of the hour I told Landsman to fuck off."

"Telling a teacher to fuck off isn't anything big?"

"I worked hard most of the whole hour."

"Yes, you did," I say.

"Anything else?"

"No, man. Why you give a shit? Nobody cares around here anyway. You just get off on this, don't you?"

Before I can think or follow procedure, I find myself saying in an unusually loud voice, "That's a lie, Jackie. It's a lie to say that no one cares here."

She seems startled by the strength behind my words, by the fact that I look her directly in the eye and that I am genuinely angry.

"Okay," she waves one hand. "Okay, Landsman. You're right."

She slumps in her seat. She is surrounded by eight adults. It is almost four o'clock, and the snow is building up outside.

"Okay, Jackie," the principal wipes his forehead. "What can you do about this?"

"I can stop calling names." She knows what to say.

"For how many days?"

"A week."

"How about trying it for two days."

"Oh, man, that's too easy."

"Let's say three." He writes her commitment into the notebook.

"Here's your bus token." He holds out his hand.

She takes the token and leaves the room, slamming the door behind her, muttering something we cannot hear.

We leave quickly. The principal calls out a "Thank you all" into the hallway. The words echo in the empty corridors.

I stand by a window in my dark classroom. I can see Jackie waiting under a streetlight on the corner, her hands cupped around a match. She moves her head up and I can see a cigarette hanging from her lips. After a moment she begins walking down the street in her high heels and tight pants.

Burt stops by for a moment on his way home, a wool cap pulled down over his head.

"That's a tough one," he says, following my gaze.

"Yeah," I say, switching off my light.

"She's not so tough," says Bill, a hall aide who has passed by the room. "You just don't like being told your pecker is small!" Burt makes a motion as if to cuff Bill along the side of the head. They put their arms around each other and walk down the hall.

Over the long weekend, I try not to think about the kids. We spend Thursday with old friends. On Saturday, Maury and I celebrate our fifteenth wedding anniversary. We go out to an expensive restaurant, drink a bottle of wine. This year we toast to our luck, to the fact that we met in the first place, braved the wrath of our parents: mine who were not pleased that Maury is a Jew, his who were just as angry that I am not Jewish.

The Monday after Thanksgiving vacation, Frankie comes up to my desk at the end of fifth hour.

"My dad needs more worksheets—for me," he says.

"Okay," I answer. "He'll need to work on the two-syllable words with you."

"Yeah." Frankie stands in front of me in those overwashed pants from his uncle. There is a section of brown skin visible between the cuffs of these pants and the socks he wears. His shoes still have no laces. I have seen him waiting for a bus wearing only a thin sweater in addition to the T-shirt he has on now.

"Why don't I give you a ride home tonight and go over these with your dad?" I ask him.

Frankie is silent for a moment. He looks at the floor. Kids are going by my doorway. Some of them call in to say hello.

"Yeah," says Frankie.

"You could call him first and see if it's all right."

"Don't got no phone," he says.

"I'll go with you anyway," I say. "Just meet me here after group."

That afternoon Frankie arrives at my door. He has on the sweater I noticed the other day, but no gloves or hat. Someone calls out "raggedy ass" as we walk by. Frankie ignores the comment. I want to say something but decide that Frankie desperately needs to avoid a scene.

Frankie is silent during the drive to his house. He fools with the radio, finds a station he likes, and leaves it there, keeping the volume quite low. So much of Minneapolis seems close to the ground, with one-story stucco houses or two-story apartment buildings lined up side by side, leaving plenty of room for sky and the long reach of dark branches. This mid-western city seems to hunker down to the earth like an animal on the prairie, keeping warm against the wind.

I stop in front of a small, one-story house. Frankie gets out quickly and walks ahead of me. He opens the front door and calls into the back of the house. "Dad?" A dog runs up to me, baring its teeth.

"Stop that," says Frankie, grabbing the dog around its neck. "It's okay, Landsman. Spiker won't hurt you none."

Frankie's father walks out from the kitchen in a white sleeveless under-shirt and dark pants, smoking a cigarette. I hold out my hand.

"Frankie said you needed some more words," I say, "so I brought them over."

"Well, thank you very much, now," says Mr. Lee. "You sit down and I'll get you somethin' to drink." He points to the only piece of furniture in the living room, a couch with cracked plastic cushions.

I take off my coat and sit down.

"Thank you," I say when Mr. Lee comes back into the room bearing a glass of orange juice. We sit side by side while I show him the next set of words. Mr. Lee's breath smells of alcohol, yet he is steadier on his feet than he was when he came to visit me at school. He sounds out the words with me. When I glance over at Frankie, I see that he is sounding out the words silently as we read. I want to tell Frankie that he has been teaching his father well, that Mr. Lee can sound out this next set of words quite effortlessly. We work for ten minutes. When I close the folder the dog is stretched out on the bare floor, asleep. Frankie leans against the wall, his eyes on me and his father.

I set the empty glass on the floor and stand up to leave. Mr. Lee holds my coat for me.

"Glad Frankie's doin' so well," he says.

"He just needs to keep coming and keep practicing and he'll be able to read the newspaper real soon."

Frankie smiles. This is the second time I've seen such a smile from him. The first was when he bowled that strike. His father nods his head and smiles, too. Their smiles are identical, except for the absence of some of Mr. Lee's front teeth.

"Thank you then," Mr. Lee says. He opens the door.

"No problem," I say. "Thanks for the juice."

Mr. Lee nods his head, turns back into the living room.

"See you tomorrow," I say to Frankie.

"Okay," he responds. He stands by the doorway after his father has disap-peared into the back of the house. I look back and see him, still in the doorway, the dog next to him. He doesn't move as I drive away.

DECEMBER

"One would want people to take the view that family life is so very important. That the lack of a close-knit family, the lack of something to hold onto, disorients people."

—Rena Wilson, grandmother to Leticia,
Before Their Time

Ice coats the streets. I drive to the Teen Age Medical Center with the students in my new women's group, the wind pushing my car from side to side. An old woman holds onto a telephone pole as she waits for a bus. A man carrying a brown paper bag, wearing three different hats, one atop another, stumbles into an entryway.

The medical center is in an old wooden house converted into offices. We are given a room that looks out on the street; three bay windows let in cold light. A radiator hisses and clangs like a stalling train engine. The room has no chairs but there is a thick carpet and lots of pillows. The girls stretch out on the floor, lean against the walls. They bend their heads in unison over cigarettes. Matches scratch and flare quickly. The feeling is not institutional but homelike.

I look around at them, at Carol with her crooked arm, at Jackie in her heels and tight jeans, and Linda, quiet, tense, but laughing at the things the other say. I wanted Sandy to come, but Rhonda wouldn't sign the permission slip. I've brought Karen along, too. She's just come back to school after a month-long absence, but now Davey is beginning to drift again. The child protection agency and Jane are trying to find out what is changing in Davey's life. Policeofficers have stopped by on the days he is gone. He is elusive, like Karen, who seems to become even thinner as the winter fattens white around us.

The pediatrician, a tough-minded older woman, begins a discussion of contraception and sexuality. She is very businesslike at first, bringing out charts and diagrams. The kids giggle and Jackie makes sure we all know that she is familiar with every device that is passed around.

"You just get him to slip this over his thing," Jackie says, holding up a condom. "But he's got to wait til his thing is all bony like some ol' elbow."

Carol stares at the condom. Linda looks away. Karen giggles. I know that this is not new to them: not the descriptions of what happens during sex or afterwards, not the discussion of diseases or the sight of a condom. They squirm in their seats and they blush, maybe because all this is being said in front of me, or maybe they are not used to this much detailed information. They want to know about my sex life: whether I "do it," whether I like it. They pass around the diaphragms, the jellies, the foam. They look at me as I handle each item.

Today I feel protective of myself. I am silent about my sex life, something of my own that these kids cannot fragment. I become quieter than usual, move away from the group just slightly.

"So, what do you do if you're horny?" asks the pediatrician.

"What?" asks Carol.

"She means, what if you don't have a man and you want to do it," says Jackie.

Carol shrugs her shoulders. "Shit. I don't know."

"You can give yourself pleasure," the doctor says. "You can touch yourself."

"That's gross," says Carol.

"No. It's very nice, actually," says the doctor.

"You do it?" asks Jackie.

"Yes, sometimes when I feel sexual but my husband isn't around."

"Oh, man," Carol says.

Karen wrinkles her nose and reaches for another cigarette.

"Ever tried the faucet?" asks Jackie.

"What you mean, the faucet?"

"I mean you sit in the bathtub and stick yourself under the faucet when it's running warm water."

"No, girl. That ain't true. You don't stick your pussy under no faucet." Karen sounds disgusted.

"Yeah, I do! And it works."

"Well, girl, I'll just go right home and try it," says Karen.

"You go ahead. You try it. Just make sure the water ain't too cold."

"Maybe I better try some of these things," Carol says. "I plan to be a virgin until I'm nineteen years old."

Jackie looks up. Before she can check herself she says, "Oh, man. I'd be so proud if I was a virgin at nineteen."

The room is quiet. Linda stares out the window. Karen twists her hair nervously against her thin face.

"I'd be so proud," Jackie repeats, more softly now.

The silence is full: of Linda wanting to push her father off her, of Karen's nighttime work in front of cameras, and of Jackie wanting to reject the first pimp who ever promised her warmth and cigarettes.

I do not try to fill in their silence. I cannot. Jackie has spoken and now they are looking at their lives with regret.

We sit for a while without speaking.

Finally, I tell them we must get back before fifth hour classes begin.

In the car they are talkative again.

At a stoplight in downtown Minneapolis, Jackie rolls down her window and yells to a young man walking across the street, "Hey

The man turns.

"Hey you! See this woman here?" She points to me. "Hey! She wants you!"

He is a slim black man dressed in a beautiful tweed over-coat and pointed shoes. I can see his maroon tie up tight next to his brown throat, his stiff pale blue collar snug around his neck. He is wearing a felt hat with a small brim and a wide ribbon. His dark glasses are turned in my direction.

I'd like to be able to crawl under the steering wheel. The light is interminably red. As we drive by the man, Jackie points to me and says again, "I mean it, sweetheart. She wants you."

He turns away, shaking his head.

She rolls up the window and looks at my red face. She laughs and so do the other girls.

"Hey, Landsman. Hey, I'm sorry," she says. But she keeps smiling.

The rest of the way back to school we listen to rock music on the radio. I'm thinking, not so much about that man on the street, but about danger, how we tempt it, how we want it sometimes, to prove something to ourselves, to others.

In D.C. while I was in college, I lived life fearlessly on night streets, walking back to my apartment at 2 A.M. I drank beer at Brownlies Bar and saw men thrown out onto their backs, landing on the sidewalk with enough force to break bones. A group of us from George Washington University worked as tutors in city schools. We marched in front of the White House and worked for voter registration in Gum Springs, Virginia, a town that housed the remnants of the slave quarters of George Washington's plantation. We made love, trading partners the way kids trade baseball cards.

I needed to risk something. I needed to escape the plans my parents had for me: a large clapboard house in Massachusetts and marriage to a doctor. I had the luxury of choosing danger. But young women like Jackie and Linda never had the choice. The kids line up in my dreams these nights.

Mid-December brings our second fifteenth anniversary. We had two weddings, a Protestant one for my parents and, three weeks later, a Jewish one for Maury's parents. Some years we get two sets of anniversary cards.

That morning kids stand outside my classroom door and watch as the delivery man brings in the box wrapped in florist paper. I unwrap red roses from Maury. Lately Maury pulls away when I begin to talk about my students. Today, I breathe in his gift gratefully.

During the morning, the kids notice the flowers. The girls say nothing, the boys talk about the strong smell in the room. At the end of fifth hour after everyone has gone, Johnny comes up to me at my desk and puts his arms around my neck, pleading like a small child, "Please, Landsman, can I please have one of these for my new lady?"

I can feel his breath against my cheek, and his skin is warm.

"Oh, Johnny. If I give you one, then everyone will know, and they'll all want one. Then what would I do?"

"I won't tell no one. I'll sneak in here right before the bus leaves and take one and hide it in my jacket and then give it to my lady when we get home." He waits, his arms resting on the back of my neck.

"Oh. Okay. After school."

Johnny grasps me tighter, kisses my cheek.

"Thank you, Landsman." He runs to get to his next class.

I am surprised at myself. I am not sure why I agreed to give him one of the roses. Maybe it's because he has become easy to have in class these days. He settles down for half an hour at a time, and his reading is so much better. Maybe it's because he caught me at a weak moment.

Later that afternoon he comes in, breathless. He chooses the rose and dashes out, keeping it under his coat just as he promised. When I look out at the buses I see him with his arm around the waist of a seventh-grade girl, guiding her up the steps in front of him. I wonder if the thorns are pushing through his shirt, if the rose will survive there, pressed up against his heart.

A few days before winter vacation, the first-hour kids relax into a discussion.

Sandy says she doesn't believe you come back as an animal after you die. You go to either heaven or hell. That's it.

Johnny says he's not so sure. He thinks maybe if you're bad you come back as an insect.

"Yeah, like Chicago is full of bad guys there," says Anthony, who has dropped in today. His fur-collared coat is draped over a chair next to him. He wears a tie and a three-piece suit.

"Why you say that?" asks Davey. "Chicago ain't a bad city. Not badder than Minneapolis."

"Oh, yeah it is. It's badder," says Anthony. "And I figure the reason they got all them roaches is because they got all the criminals after they died. They got so many roaches. Chicago must be full of dead criminals."

Jackie laughs. When she laughs, everyone does. The whole class laughs about Chicago and the roaches.

Johnny says, suddenly, "What you think is going to happen when the man that shot Martin Luther King dies?"

"Man, he got to come back as some ant. And the first black person walking by gets to squash him," says Anthony, rubbing his hands together.

"Yeah," says Johnny, satisfied.

At lunch I tell the other teachers about this conversation. We laugh, yet each one of us, black and white, remember King, the sixties, what we were doing when he died. And each one of us understands Johnny's satisfaction at the thought of James Earl Ray, squashed flat.

In 1965 at the end of King's march from Selma, Alabama, a group of us from D.C. went by train to join the end of the march into Montgomery. When it grew dark we made our way back to the small platform at the rear of the train. The scent of honeysuckle and lilac was so sweet and heavy I wanted to lick it off my fingers. We sang old civil rights songs, then marching songs, hymns, love songs. We sang loudly so that all of Virginia, Mississippi, and Alabama would hear us, would know we were coming.

In Montgomery, we walked and sang and danced down the middle of the street. Civil rights workers, black and white, dressed in coveralls and red bandannas, joined us, coming from the basements of churches along the dusty roads where a collection of shacks leaned into each other in the middle of a field. White store owners stood on the corners and lit cigarettes, one after another. Some had eyes that seemed to be pulled into slits in their faces. Others stared absently past our heads. Their hands twisted and turned in front of them. Women stood among them, watching. These women seemed to me to be thin as cats. Some pinned their hair close to their heads with bobby pins crisscrossed against their skulls, while others wore loose ponytails or tall beehives glinting with hair spray. They took notes with their eyes, watching everyone and where they went, who followed our dancing line and who stayed back. Some shook their heads. A few smiled hesitantly. One man spat on the ground in front of us as we went by.

We could feel the whole city waiting through the on-coming evening and into the next day. They knew we were headed back to D.C., New York, Connecticut. Montgomery, Alabama bided its time, while we danced and drifted in a changing, fluid rearrangement of bodies.

After the speeches on the Capitol mall, the march broke up. We were frightened for the people we left behind, turning for home, away from the large houses of their bosses, walking back toward their section of town, alone on dirt roads.

Now I feel a similar fear for my kids when the weekend comes. In 1965 I got on that train and headed back to D.C. In Minneapolis, I head home on Friday evening to dinner, maybe a movie, to Maury's face, his steady breathing. My kids are on the streets. These days I feel I betray them by going home.

The winter weather brings the students into school more often. Carol with her crooked arm, Anthony in his fur coat, Davey with his sidekick Karen, and Jackie sporting her flimsy clothes and high heels are around more, and they are full of stories. I need time to work on reading materials away from the kids. I hide out in the library during my prep hour these days. One Tuesday morning while I grade worksheets, the librarian rushes over and asks if I know where Linda is this hour.

"She's in typing," I say. "Do you want me to get her?"

"Her father's here."

"What?" I whisper. "Where is he?"

"Upstairs, near your room."

Linda is not supposed to see her father. I had thought him safely locked up until his trial.

I hurry up the stairs to find him leaning against the wall outside my classroom door, a man with pink cheeks and hair plastered to his head. He wears a short army jacket and blue jeans.

"Can I help you?" I ask.

He sways as he tries to stand.

"Yeah. You can get me my daughter."

He moves his hand toward the inside of his worn jacket.

Ted Marvin is walking toward us. He can see what's happening and ducks into his office to make the necessary phone call.

"I don't think she's supposed to see you." I say this as calmly as I can. I'm trembling, from hatred as much as from fear.

"Don't tell me about my own girl," he says, leaning back against the wall.

At this moment Linda comes up the stairs and turns the corner. When she sees her father she pales and flattens herself against the lockers. He spots her and tries to move around me, his hand still in his jacket.

Ted has come into the hallway. He steps between Linda and her father.

"Mr. Owens. You'll have to leave."

"I'll leave with Linda," he says.

"No." Linda's voice is strong. "No, you won't."

She begins to cry. Two more principals come down the hall from the other direction.

Linda takes a step toward her father.

"I can't, Dad. Don't you see?"

He lunges for her but falls against the wall.

I unlock the door to my room and signal to Linda. She slips in and I close it quickly behind us. She stands in the middle of the room and puts her hands over her face. I go over to her and hold her.

When the bell rings and the kids begin to assemble for fourth hour, they stop quickly at the sight of me holding Linda. I'm not sure she will ever stop crying.

Johnny leads everyone back out into the hallway. They wait until I call them into the room.

The hour is subdued. Linda sits next to my desk. No one says much. After about twenty minutes I leave the rest of them to continue on their own and take Linda to Jane. I return to my room after I'm sure that Linda is calm. The kids know that something has happened, and that it's difficult for me to talk. For the first time all year, Johnny does not ask me for help.

Jackie stops by on her way home later in the afternoon.

"Heard about Linda."

"She'll be okay now," I say.

"Sure. Okay." Jackie doesn't leave, waiting beside my desk.

"Her dad came after her?" she asks.

"Yeah." I can't say more.

"Men are fucks," says Jackie.

I am quiet. I want to say, "Not all men," but I don't. The statement hangs between us, though.

"You like men, Landsman?" Jackie asks, turning toward me, staring intently. She is chewing gum, and the mint smell wafts toward me.

"I like some men," I say. "I like my husband. And my son."

"I like some, too. Sometimes." Jackie offers me a piece of her gum.

Although it's late, Sandy comes in now to ask, "How is Linda?"

"I think she'll be okay."

"Heard about it from Johnny," Sandy says, settling back on her heels, her arms folded across her chest. "They shouldn't let that ol' man out on the streets!"

She is indignant, righteous.

"I heard that!" Jackie offers Sandy gum. We all sit, chewing, thinking.

"Men," says Sandy, shaking her head. She says the word as though it is a complete sentence.

Jackie nods. "All those men out there," she says.

The two girls get up at the same time. Sandy waits until Jackie has slipped on her jean jacket. She puts on her own dark purple wool coat.

"Say hello to Rhonda," I say, realizing that I haven't heard from Sandy's aunt in a while.

"I will, Landsman."

"You see your mom?" I ask Jackie.

"Not since I moved into the group home last week."

I nod.

"You like it there?" asks Sandy.

"It's okay." Jackie shrugs her shoulders. She heads toward the door.

"See ya, Landsman," she says.

"See ya." I smile.

She returns the smile, timidly. "You know, Landsman, I think you got to be crazy to work in a place like this! All these sorry kids and they sorry fathers."

"Yeah, maybe. Maybe that's how I got the job. I like it, though," I answer.

"I don't think she's *totally* crazy," says Sandy.

"Not yet," says Jackie. "Just wait." They both laugh. I join them, a little nervousness in my laughter.

When I get home, Aaron is sitting in the living room fooling with some new music on his electric guitar. The sun on his pale skin makes it appear even whiter than its usual winter pallor. He barely looks up when I sit beside him on the couch. I want to tell him about Linda, about her father. I find I can't talk. I sit. I listen to Aaron's scattered music. I pull a blanket around me and fall asleep.

When I wake up, Aaron has gone to his room. I wake to the memory of Linda's face as she edges against the locker. I felt that intensity of fear once, just once. She has lived with it all her life.

Maury comes in, snowflakes on his glasses and beard. He stamps his feet, takes off his boots, and hangs up his coat. I do not tell him about Linda. I have no energy left. I reach up. He bends toward me. His beard is wet against my cheek.

The week before winter vacation is always the toughest one of all. The kids are excited, angry, and frightened. They pace the room and fight in the halls. They are eager to be out of school but are also nervous about having so much time at home.

I plan something different for each day of the week. I take them sledding one afternoon, show a movie the next, arrange a spelling bee on Wednesday and a storytelling contest on Thursday. On the last day before winter break I bring the young women together for a party during our women's class. They provide the food: chips and dip, pop, cookies. We sit around and talk.

Carol yells to Jackie. "Hey! Remember what you said about putting your pussy under the faucet?"

I run over and shut the door.

"Yeah," Jackie answers.

"Well. I tried it and it doesn't work."

"You try it, Landsman?" Jackie asks.

Before I say anything, Carol jumps in, "She don't need to try it. She got her husband." The two of them laugh and Sandy looks bewildered.

Carol stares out the window, her crooked shoulder aslant in her blue shirt. She turns to the girls. "You ever see your mom?" she asks.

"I see my aunt every night when I go home," says Sandy.

"Nope. I don't. Not anymore," says Jackie.

"Nope," says Linda. "My mom gave me to my grandmother, and my grandmother gave me to my aunt. Then my aunt sent me to my dad. And now I'm in the shelter."

"I try not to see too much of my mom," says Karen, sockless as usual.

"Why you want to know?" asks Jackie.

"I just started living with my aunt' cause my mom went to live on the res."

"You miss her?" asks Jackie.

Carol shrugs.

"What that mean?" asks Sandy, imitating Carol's shrug.

"Oh. I' spose I don't miss her."

"You' spose. You either miss her or you don't miss her!" says Sandy, who has raised her body up to that straight-backed position that means trouble.

"Okay. I do miss her," Carol says. She sits up straight, imitating Sandy.

"That's right," says Sandy, smiling and relaxing in her chair. "We all miss our mothers."

"Not me," says Karen, chewing on her nails.

"You got to miss her somewhere inside you," says Sandy.

"Nope." Karen shrugs her thin shoulders. One side of her sweatshirt slips down, exposing a dirty bra strap.

"I miss mine," says Jackie. "I think you always miss your mom. You always want her."

After a moment Sandy says, "I know that's right."

"You miss her when something happens to you. Like when I broke my arm," says Carol. "Oooooh, it hurt, girl."

"Yeah. You miss her when you get hurt," Jackie says. "Like when a man got me in the basement of Derrick's building. He just threw bottles at me down there' til I couldn't go nowhere." Jackie stares straight ahead as she talks.

"Ooooh, girl. That so cold."

"When was that?" asks Karen, sucking on the sleeve of her shirt.

"Last summer."

"When you living over on 12th?"

"Yeah."

"You didn't tell nobody?"

"No. Wasn't nobody to tell. Derrick wouldn't have believed me."

"What about your mother, then?" I ask.

"My mother don't ever believe me," she says, her voice hard, a statement of fact.

"Mothers," says Sandy.

"Men," says Karen.

"Mothers and men," says Carol, shaking her head.

"What you gonna do?" says Jackie with false cheerfulness, breaking the mood.

Carol gets up and collects paper plates. Linda brushes crumbs off the table. Sandy pours leftover soda into a drinking fountain across from my room. Jackie searches her purse for gum, cigarettes, change for the bus.

They finish cleaning up. After the bell rings Sandy stays back for a moment.

"Some days," she asks me, "you ever just feel like weepin'?"

"Yes. Lots of days."

She nods her head and walks out the door.

The halls are quiet. The kids have all left. Jackie is headed to the group home, Sandy to church, Karen to Davey, who waits for her by the fountain downtown, Linda to the shelter, and Carol to her aunt's house in the projects. None of them live with their mothers right now.

And yet each of these kids still wants her mother's blessing.

Heading home for two weeks of winter break, I think how cold the wind is that blows at me as I unlock my car, how Karen has no socks.

WINTER BREAK

It is snowing. I have time for lunches with friends; I enjoy the incredible luxury of time to eat slowly, time to stay for an extra cup of coffee. At home in the evenings, we light Hanukkah candles. Maury chants a prayer in Hebrew. The Christmas tree lights blink in the front windows. Aaron is unusually quiet; he sleeps late most mornings. His friends come over in the afternoons, bringing snow in on their tennis shoes. Like their mothers, I gave up insisting on boots years ago. Aaron buys his clothes at secondhand stores. He pins up the bottom of his pants with safety pins. He has talked about dying his hair blue. I loved the six months when he went through his preppy phase: button-down shirts and crewneck sweaters. Yet, when he pierced one ear, wore old plaid shirts and zip-down sweaters, I bit my lip. Maury held his tongue.

The day after Christmas, Lesley, Walter, and their three-year-old daughter, Carey, come to spend a few days.

Lesley and I are the oldest two children of five. We have kept a strong connection that has to do with the pull of a common childhood, memories of safety, our early years in Connecticut. For a while Lesley lived with a man in New York City who went crazy; he threatened her with a knife while they were in his car on Riverside Drive. She jumped out and never went back to their apartment, not even to get her things. Later she organized welfare workers in Upper New York State and was chased away at gunpoint because she rode in a car with a black man. During her years of law school, she shared a house with George Wiley, a welfare rights activist. Often, she'd come home to find that someone had broken into the house, ransacked his files, left money untouched, the TV still in the corner, the silverware in rows on the sideboard.

Now she lives in West Lafayette with Walter, a small-town Indiana man. When he came home from Vietnam, he divorced his first wife and would not talk about the war.

I want to like the man she has married, yet I find it difficult. Walter has managed to live his married life as though he is a single man. Lesley does the cooking and most of the child care. She has lost some of her toughness around him, has become the exhausted lawyer, wife, mother—the one who does it all. She is pregnant with her second child. And yet, despite my frustration with their relationship, there are things about Walter I like: his sense of humor, his populist politics, his laughter.

The mornings they are here we drink coffee and talk until noon. Walter is trying different diets because his stomach is troubling him. In the afternoons, Les and I take Carey to movies or, on an unusually warm day, sledding at the golf course. In the evenings we find more to talk about, Les and I reminiscing about D.C. or New York.

When Lesley leaves, I become restless. Even though it feels good to have the mornings to myself again, the house quiet, Aaron asleep downstairs, I miss her with an ache that surprises me.

I have just read a story about a woman who was dragged from her wheel-chair, raped, and tied back into the wheelchair. I wish Lesley were still here. I receive Christmas cards from the five women I lived with in D.C. one sum-mer. I am having dreams about the house we all shared, but in this house I see Jackie and Linda, and I know that Linda's father is nearby. I am pinned against a wall by a man whose face I have wanted to forget. I would like Lesley here while I remember. It is hard to do this alone.

Now I write it out, the story I have been trying not to remember. One summer, when I had to take an extra course and needed a place to stay, I found a room in Dick and Ellie Yeo's house. Dick was the minister who ran the office where much of our political activity took place. Maury was in D.C., too, helping out in his father's liquor store. He was living with his parents, saving money for Yale graduate school.

Dick's house was across from a deserted circle full of beautiful flowers. His back porch faced an alley that was a hangout for the small children who lived in a row of rundown houses around the corner. In D.C., elegant homes were often located one block away from streets where men walked around with blood running from their faces, where old women sat on rotting porches and watched grandchildren step carefully over bottles. A half-mile away from the house where I lived that summer, the white towers on the Potomac could be seen behind the lower buildings.

I write: One hot afternoon a man came into Dick's house through a screen door someone had left open. I was there alone in my room in the attic. I had taken aspirin for cramps and was trying to nap. I fell into a light sleep in that hot room, dimly hearing women yelling at their children just below my window. I woke, turned over on my back, and saw a man standing in the doorway. He wore a white T-shirt, black pants, and sneakers. In his left hand was a knife. The silver blade caught afternoon sunlight, the light dancing around the room every time he waved it at me. He looked startled when I sat up, my back against the headboard of the bed. I pulled the single sheet over my T-shirt and shorts. Then his face became expressionless. He came forward into the room. Without a word, he pulled at my wrist with his free hand until

I was standing. I could feel a fresh flow of blood move from between my legs, the cramps easing up. For a moment I was concerned about whether I would leak, about whether my underwear would become stained.

He kept hold of my wrist, pulling me from room to room. He had me load things into a paper bag: radios, silverware, clothes, jewelry. He never spoke, using the knife as a pointer. He jerked me roughly from the attic to the second floor, then the first floor. Winnie, the family dog, lay under the sideboard, blood pouring from her head.

He pulled me all the way back upstairs to my room. The afternoon silence was broken only by a truck stopping for a delivery in the alley, a man calling for someone to open a door.

When we got to my room, the man pointed to the bed. I sat down. He pointed to my finger. I slipped off the garnet ring from my mother, the amethyst pinky ring from my grandmother. He stood above me while I pulled them off, my hands shaking, my body trembling.

He pushed me back on the bed and pulled at my shorts. I slipped them off, terrified of making him angry. He pulled at my underwear. I slipped them off, too. He pulled his own pants down. He put the knife on the table next to my head. I could see it out of the corner of my eye.

I write: He climbed over me and put his cock into my mouth. He put his hand behind my neck and pushed and pulled my head so that my mouth would move over him. When he became hard, he pulled out of my mouth and moved down over my body. He pushed himself into me, moved in and out of my body.

I write this. I am sitting in Minneapolis, and my son sleeps downstairs. I write this, and the kids, Jackie and Linda and Carol, are somewhere in this city.

The man moved out of me. He pulled up his pants and took some rope out of his pocket. Neither of us had spoken a word.

"Please don't kill me," I said.

He tied my wrists to the headboard. While he was doing this, while the ropes cut into my skin, the knife lay, like something animate, right near my head.

Then, in a gesture I will never understand, he pulled the sheet up over my partially nude body and left me there, bleeding.

I did not try to move, afraid the groan of the bedsprings would bring him back. I could hear the dog whimpering downstairs.

I was not sure for awhile if I was alive. I lay perfectly still while the blood dried on the sheets, while the sweat rolled down my neck and breasts. My muscles ached, each one rigid. I could hear the sounds of children on the street behind the house, fighting with each other, riding the sidewalks on squeaky tricycles. I listened for his footsteps on the stairs, terrified he would appear again at the doorway, knife in hand, startled to see me there. My body tightened more and more, each muscle knotting up.

I write: I pulled my wrists away from the bed, loosening the ropes. As I pulled, the rope burned my skin. I continued to pull until I had loosened them enough to bring my hands in front of my face. I worked at the knots, my fingers spastic, out of control. Suddenly, I noticed that there was no sound coming from the street below, no children, no delivery man, no women. I wondered if he was out there, if he was walking the alley with his paper bag, if everyone had hurried inside. I stopped moving. I waited, listening for his step again. I only heard the dog Winnie and her pain.

Suddenly, a man's voice drifted from the alley into the room where I lay. "You get on in the house, Lakita. Your mama got sausages for you now."

I stood up, wrapping the sheet around the lower half of my body. I moved awkwardly downstairs to Dick and Ellie's bedroom, where there was a phone. I walked the way a little girl walks when she is playing dress-up. There on the bureau he had rummaged through Ellie's jewelry and had me load her rings, bracelets, and necklaces into the bag. My whole body could not stop shaking, bleeding. I dialed the liquor store where Maury was working. I was surprised at how calm I sounded when I asked for him.

I write this. The dog sleeps in the sun at my feet. Aaron will be up soon. When Maury came to the phone I sobbed into the receiver, "I've been raped, I've been raped." I couldn't stop saying it. I couldn't stop crying it. Maury said he'd be right over. His voice sounded remote across the city.

As I was talking to Maury, as he was trying to calm me down, I looked out the window and saw my friend Barbara walking across the circle. I told Maury I had to get off, that Barbara was coming. I hung up, opened the window and called to her. I went downstairs, still wrapped in my sheet, and opened the door for her. The dog was whimpering behind me. I cried. I asked Barb to touch my shoulders, my bruised wrists. Barb held me. She led me back upstairs and sat me on the bed while she dialed the police. She held my hand, turned it over in her hand, noticed the red burns.

In five minutes the police descended on the house, blue uniforms in every room. They asked me questions and then waited for me to put my clothes in a bag for them. They drove me to the emergency room. Maury had arrived in the middle of their questioning and rode with me in the back of the squad car. The two policewomen who drove us talked recipes, about whether to use honey or molasses. In the hospital while I was being examined, a man in the cubicle next to me moaned and swore as the nurses worked on him. I remember wanting to be sick when I heard his voice because he sounded angry, out of control, and this frightened me. On the way back to Dick's house, riding in the back of the squad car again, Maury put his arms around me and held me close. The women in front talked about a party that weekend, about whether to bring beer or soda, what to eat, what to do if it rained.

Do these memories return because Lesley has come and gone, because Sandy and Linda and Jackie are looking for safety? I reword the story, hoping that this process will lessen the pain: A man came. He did not speak. He brought silver in one hand that hurt the edges of my eyes. He took my garnet ring, my amethyst ring. He pushed into me with his body. The dog whimpered but she survived that day.

These words do not change anything. I see the city and that place, and I remember the evening, after being at the emergency room.

After Maury and I arrived back at my room, I showered and changed my clothes, and he drove me to a liquor store to pick up some Champale. Then I asked him to take me straight into the arms of the women I had spent the last year with, to Barbara, Marie, Marty, Stacy, and Jeanie.

Champale was the rage that summer. It tasted like beer with a touch of champagne. The name sounded like the color of a blouse, a kind of off-white with a touch of beige. I put the six-pack in the refrigerator.

Before that night we had not really noticed all the places where men could hide, the dark bushes, the corners of the bridge, the steep drop below. We had walked around the streets that year assuming our bodies were our own. We held our books next to our chests as we headed home from class; walked two miles in the dark of Washington, past a million places where a man with a knife—slim instrument of fear—could hide. We were casual. We had come and gone from the house in Georgetown, barely aware of each other's presence, leaving notes, checks toward the phone bill, requests for household items.

That night there was absolutely nothing to say. Stacy curled up with me, knowing that she would move out and into the evening differently. Jeanie sat on the floor, a stream of moonlight resting on her blue-black hair, and Marty sat on a rocking chair, a beer on the floor next to her, pulling cigarette after cigarette out of the package. Barbara stretched out on her bed. Her tears moved back onto the pillow and into her hair.

Maury left, walking softly out of the room. Something was wrong with his presence right then. There was something out of place about his muscular chest, the mat of hair showing in the V of his shirt. Something frightening about his back. He left knowing that his life had changed, too.

And finally, as the night came into the room and we drank Champale, I cried because my tears were the only things I could call my own. I cried because Stacy had fallen asleep, her blond head on my chest, her body hurting me as it pushed up against my bruised rib. I wanted my own mother, but I didn't think I could tell her what had happened, and now there would be a wall between us at just the wrong time in my life.

As the summer night came in at the windows, we all cried because we loved each other and because loving each other wasn't enough.

Remembering that night, I think about the kids, lying on those pillows at the Teen Age Medical Center, Jackie wishing she was a virgin. There was a feeling of helplessness in that room, too, of not being able to do anything to change the ugly way of the world.

In the women's group I tell them to protect themselves, to stay off the streets after dark, to go places together. I tell them that no one, no matter what time of day or night, has the right to touch them. Yet I also say, don't put yourselves in danger. They nod their heads, but I know they will not change the evenings they go to parties with no ride home, or nights spent outside, near the lake, with no home to go to. I hope Jackie will be safe, yet I know she could find herself in some dark basement again, a man trapping her in the corner.

The day after I was raped, the police asked me to come down to the station and fill out a report. Maury had driven me there and was waiting for me in the hallway, seated alone on a large bench. I sat across from a woman who typed my story in a high-ceilinged room full of women and their typewriters. As I described what happened, how he came into my room, how he led me around the house, how he tied me up, all the other typewriters stopped and all of the women listened, their hands poised above the keys, their foreheads wrinkled in concentration, straining to hear my words. In that warm room I could see small damp patches under their arms. Most of them looked to be in their forties or fifties, their eyes revealing a hunger for the details. They did not try to hide the fact that they were fascinated by my story.

After I recounted the entire rape, the words coming automatically, without emotion, I was shown into a back room where a policeman took my fingerprints. When he was finished he motioned for me to bend close to him to listen to something confidential, something just between the two of us. I don't remember what he looked like, except that he was overweight.

"That your boyfriend?" he asked, gesturing toward the hallway where Maury was sitting.

"Yes," I answered, frightened.

"Well, honey," the cop drawled in a slow southern accent, "you just find yourself another young man, and when you do, you don't tell him anything about this. Then he won't know what happened. He won't know you're damaged."

I got up and walked out of the office, stiff with shock, anger, and that awful self-doubt that somehow I was responsible, that somehow I had invited this man with his knife into my room.

In the car, I told Maury what the cop had said. There were no words that would help; only his touch, his tears, and the overwhelming anger we had both begun to feel.

After he left me off at the apartment where I was staying with my women friends, Maury went back to his father's liquor store. Later he told me that he had been sick in the small toilet near the cases of beer. We had been going together for over a year, were rarely apart in the evenings. He sensed that this would change. And he was right.

The next day, and for days afterwards, even though he and I spent time together, it was women I wanted curled up around me in the room as the morning came slowly, the only cool time of day in D.C. I wanted them breathing next to me so the whole room moved up and down to that rhythm, their white arms resting on their nightgowns, their legs at odd angles, their mouths slightly open.

Women were my sanity, soft voices at night, questions in the morning, someone pouring me orange juice.

I called home to tell mother that my rings had been stolen. She sounded worried.

"Oh, sweetie, suppose you had been there. You might have gotten hurt."

I kept my story up near my throat. It almost escaped into the silence. I am not sure what made me so afraid to tell her. Maybe she'd say something about my civil rights work. My mother and father had never wanted me to come to George Washington University. I couldn't bear the thought that this episode proved them right, that I had brought this on myself by leaving the safety of their part of the country.

I don't know what gave me the strength not to tell her when I so much wanted her to know. I think now that it must have been my blind instinct for self-preservation. I worried that if my father found out he would insist on taking me home, away from D.C., a city he hated. And I knew that Washington,

D.C., was the place where I had to stay. It may have been a mistake not to tell them. I don't know. I knew then only that I was surrounded by people who loved me. There, in D.C., willing to come when I called, was Maury. There was touch. I simply told my mother that I was all right. I asked her not to think about it. I was fine.

I remember Jackie's words: "You always want to be with your mother." I think of children who go back to the parents who beat them. They still cry for their cruel yet familiar mothers, even after they are taken to safe places, the bruises visible on their bodies. I think about the strength of that pull, about Jackie's loneliness, about my own. I write: "Here was touch." I want Jackie to have what I had: the company of women, a place of safety—things she doesn't have.

I go out on cross-country skis. The weather is perfect: new snow, twenty degrees, and sunshine. I move back and forth by the river, working up a sweat, my silk long underwear sticking to my back. It is two in the afternoon, and traffic is almost nonexistent. A man plays with his Labrador retriever. A woman pulls her child on a sled, a small bag of groceries tucked in beside the figure in a snowsuit. I feel each muscle relax.

Later, I am driving down Hennepin Avenue on my way to meet Maury for dinner. I drive past adult bookstores and notice the pale green light inside. A few men lean against the doorway. A young woman in a short skirt stands in the middle of the block. A car slows down. She walks into the street. She leans in at the window, her dark hair falling over her face. The tires squeal as the car pulls away. She laughs and moves back on to the sidewalk. It is not Jackie. I am relieved. I've been seeing her face in my mind all week. I want to tell her what I've learned over all these years: that none of us is damaged goods.

Sandy's Aunt Rhonda calls on Sunday, the day before school starts.

"Jus' wanted you to know, she read the Bible tonight in church for the first time."

"Why, that's great. How did she sound?"

"She was slow, but she got all the words right. And everyone was so pleased they jus' yes-sistered her all the way through it."

FEBRUARY

"There are basic truths [in our neighborhoods]
about the vulnerability and power of coming
to know, about the way the world invites
and denies language."

—Mike Rose, *Lives on the Boundary*

One Saturday night, Maury and I pull up to the house at midnight after a costume party. Maury wears a wing on his left shoulder; my wing is on the right
shoulder. We were left and right wing deviationists at a party hosted by some
radical lawyer friends that featured plenty of beer, wine, and great tapes of
music from the fifties and sixties. There is nothing like dancing to leave your
body pleasantly tired. The song "My Girl," by the Temptations, plays over and
over again in my mind.

On February 2nd, after school, Jill and I visit Jackie's group home, a large
stucco house with a broad porch that extends across the entire front. The
hooks on each side of the porch will support wooden swings when the snow
thaws at the end of April.

The living room reminds me of the one at the Teen Age Medical Center.
Large pillows cover the floor and two old couches are backed against the walls.
Twelve girls live here, all of them prostitutes or runways, all under seventeen
years of age. The young woman in charge during the day leads us back through
the dining room and into the kitchen. We hear footsteps, doors banging, and
music playing upstairs. The front door opens and closes regularly.

"Coffee?" asks Sarah. She is young, in her twenties, dressed in blue jeans
and a flannel shirt. She is pretty, with dark curly hair and dark eyes.

"Thanks," we say, accepting the coffee.

"None of the girls like coffee much," says Sarah. "Nice to have some
company when I drink it." She smiles.

"How's Jackie doing?" asks Jill. She keeps on her coat. The back of the
house is chilly, and Jill told me this morning that she felt another cold coming
on.

"She's tough," Sarah says, sitting down now, putting a plate of cookies in
front of us. "I think she wants to try it, but she fights us all the way here."

"Real fistfights? Or mouthing back?" I ask.

"Mostly her mouth. She just hates our rules."

"Does she do her chores?"

"Oh, yeah. She's fine with that. She just hates it when we won't let her
old boyfriend visit, or when we make her come in on time."

"You think she'll be able to stay here?" I ask.

"I hope so," says Sarah. "I hope so. You see, we all like Jackie. I mean
there's something about her to really like."

I know what Sarah means. I also know that Sarah has worked with many troubled young women. Although she says she hopes that Jackie will stay, her voice sounds unsure, tenuous. I know that Jackie is right on the edge. But we've sensed this. And we've worked with kids like Jackie enough to trust our own uncertainty, to protect ourselves against our own sense of failure should Jackie run away or blow the rules. And we hope that our uncertainty doesn't show, that Jackie feels our support, knows that we are on her side. For some reason, this child, this girl, has touched a place within me that is especially vulnerable. There are students who, whatever the reasons, get to us more than others.

"I like her too," I say to Sarah, who is refilling her coffee cup. "I worry about the influence of her ex-boyfriend, her old crowd."

"They're definitely around," says Sarah, shaking her head. "They're always hangin' out in the yard across the street, or sitting on the porch, even in the cold."

"Does she talk to them?"

"Some. Not much. She's trying. She really is."

Jill pulls her coat tighter, shivering from a sudden internal chill.

We talk a little longer, ask Sarah to get in touch with us if there is anything more we can do. Sarah promises to call. On the porch we meet Jackie hurrying in.

"What you doin' here?" she asks, not hostile but curious.

"Just checking up on you," I say, smiling.

She returns the smile. "What you find out?"

"You're doing okay."

"Yep. Curfew sucks, though."

"Just hang in there."

"Sure, Landsman, I will."

I feel relieved as I drive home. Not that anything about Jackie is guaranteed. But right now, this week, she is safer here than she was on the streets or in her own home.

Anthony loves wearing his pimp clothes. He dresses in old, double-breasted suits, wide felt hats, and pointed shoes. He carries a cane some days until the principal tells him to leave it at home, because it "constitutes a dangerous weapon." In between classes, I often see Anthony downstairs on the one pay phone that students are allowed to use. He strikes a pose, leans toward the wall, cups his hand over the receiver.

During class one day at the beginning of February, I ask Robert to work with Anthony on some flash cards. For the first time Robert refuses a request from me.

"I don't get mixed up with no real pimp types," he says.

Anthony smiles as though pleased.

Jackie offers to help. She listens to Anthony sound out words as fast as he can. Anthony likes the stopwatch she uses. He says he can bring me a nice silver one if I want it. I tell him thanks, but no thanks.

Robert moves to a desk near the window, separated from the others. He opens up his book and works apart from the class.

Watching Anthony struggle with words in the silence of the room, I want to keep him with me, so I offer him a deal.

"If you come to class every day for two weeks, I'll take this whole first hour out to lunch," I tell him. "And no fights."

"Two weeks all at once?" he asks.

"Yep," I say.

"Come on, man," says Mitchell. "You can do that. She didn't say you have to come to school for two weeks. Just this class."

"Where we have her take us, Sandy?" asks Jackie. "We get her to take us to The Steak House?"

"How about Murray's downtown?"

"Yeah, with the fancy seats."

I laugh. "It won't be anywhere so expensive," I say. "Anyway, Anthony has to make it first."

"Oh, man, you better make it," says Robert, glowering at Anthony from across the room. There is silence for a split second after this. The bell rings.

The first week of the deal Anthony misses one day, Friday. I tell him he has to start over again.

"That's dog, man," he says to me. "That's dog. I had to see about some business. You probably don't want to pay up anyway."

"Try me and see."

Robert stares at Anthony. Anthony shrugs his shoulders. He's wearing a new sealskin coat with a mink collar. Match-sticks are lined up in the brim of his dark green hat.

On February 24th, the tenth school day in a row, Anthony walks into first hour. Not only has he come to class all ten days, but he has worked hard at his reading. The kids cheer as he sits down with a flourish, takes off his hat, brushes it with the tip of his fingers, and rolls up his sleeves. Even Robert smiles from his place across the room. I hand out permission slips to everyone.

Monday, third hour, my class heads out toward the parking lot for Anthony's lunch. He leads us down the hall, fur up around his neck. Marge Simpson, a teacher from the regular school whom I've invited to come along, looks a little uncertain as we stand around in the cold. Kids watch from the school windows.

Sandy looks fierce, stiff in her high heels and long wool coat. She refuses to say hello. Robert is wearing a good pair of pants and a sport jacket but turns his back on the rest of the students. He leans against the hood of a car next to mine. Jackie has dressed up too—in high glass heels, a low-cut pink blouse, and skin-tight black pants. She is wearing her short, light wool jacket with the fur collar. Mitchell has on the same mismatched outfit he wore to the dancing contest and an extra large sweatshirt over the whole thing. Johnny is hopping all over the place in high heeled shoes and a leather jacket.

Without the structure of school around them, the world seems uncertain, and they talk in unnaturally loud voices.

We drive to a Perkins restaurant. It is one step up from McDonalds and features a real menu. The kids want to put some tables together. One look at my class and the manager, a young kid with acne, hustles to fix up a single long row of tables for all of us.

I arrange myself at the head, Marge moves to the other end. Sandy sits next to me, and Anthony sits on my other side. The rest of the kids move in between us. Anthony looks around him, his eyes moving nervously from one person to another. He fingers the silverware next to his plate. I have never seen him so uncomfortable. He doesn't appear this ill at ease even when he struggles with words and the rest of the class is quiet enough so that everyone can hear his mistakes.

The waitress takes orders. Some kids ask for chicken dinners, others for hamburgers. Anthony cannot read the menu. He looks at me, helpless. I ask him what he wants. He says, "Chicken, just like that chicken with those potatoes." He points to a picture on the large plastic menu.

"Well, just tell her that then."

The waitress is getting closer. She dips her stiff, sprayed head down next to Anthony.

"And what can I get you?" she asks.

He says, "Just that chicken, there." He points to the photograph on the menu again.

"Okay," she says, writing on her pad.

"And what kind of dressing on your salad?"

"Yeah," says Anthony, nodding, sweat on his forehead.

"No, man, she didn't ask you do you want salad, she asked what kind of dressin'," Johnny says.

"What's that, salad?" he asks, twisting a napkin in his lap. The waitress looks down at the floor.

I expect the usual jeers, taunts, the slaps on the knee, Awman. . . .

But this is Anthony's day, and Robert says, quietly, from across the table, "He'll have French dressin' on the salad, right man?"

"Yeah, man, French dressin'," says Anthony.

I can feel us all breathe easier. The rest of the orders are taken, and the kids talk in subdued, uncomfortable tones.

"Did you have a nice weekend, Landsman?" asks Sandy.

"Why, yes, thanks, it was fine," I say. She has never asked me about my weekend before. "How about you?"

"Oh, just fine," says Sandy.

The kids play with their silverware.

"Well, where's the grub?" asks Anthony.

"You got to wait, man," Johnny says quietly.

Jackie leaves to go to the bathroom. I figure she's heading for a smoke.

When the food finally arrives, I relax. Just a moment before, I thought that maybe this lunch was not going to work, that I should have ordered in from McDonalds, or a pizza place, and had the celebration in our room.

But later, as I drive them back to the school building, I decide that the lunch outing was important for the class and for me. As the meal went on, I noticed that Jackie looked quite sedate, even demure. All of them behaved like guests. It was good for me to see them in another setting. I was pleased to see that they respected each other, or maybe me, or maybe simply being in a public place. Perhaps I was seeing that they respected themselves.

In my car, Anthony puts his arm along the backseat behind Jackie. She smiles at him and moves up next to him, laying her head on his chest. No one says much, except when we get to the school parking lot. Then each one comes to me separately and says thank you for the lunch and holds out a hand. I shake each hand before heading back to my room. By the time I pass the pay phone in the hallway, Anthony is already talking to someone. I hear him say as I go by, "French dressin', man, you know, what you got to put on a salad."

As I drive home that night, I think about how I was brought up, what I was expected to know. I came home each night to a perfectly groomed house, knowing what to say and how to eat meals with many courses.

The summer I was raped, my mother and I talked about clothes, about place mats, the flowers in the field below the patio. I didn't tell her about Maury, my Jewish lover, or about the children playing by the railroad station in D.C. The summer after I was raped, I came home and we talked about shoes, the length of skirts, and the penny candy on sale at the Country Store in Edgartown. We talked about salads and had lunch at a small restaurant by the harbor.

The smell of Jackie's perfume is still sweet in the back of my car. I remember her curled next to Anthony on the way back from the restaurant. I don't know what she needs or how to help her get whatever it is, but I sense that she needs more talk, about makeup, about Derrick, about french fries, about that day in the basement, the glass shattering around her.

After work, Maury meets me at the door with a carrot in his hand. He sets the carrot down, takes me in his arms, and we move to the music of Smokey Robinson and the Miracles. We dance out of the dining room, the table full of Aaron's schoolbooks, the red plastic sunglasses and the blue-rimmed ones, the assorted bandannas.

MARCH

"Periodically, a young drug dealer . . . will circle the school in a BMW or Mercedes . . . Temptation travels with smoked windows and fur seats; temptation wears a beeper and a gold chain braided as thick as a marine rope."

—Samuel Freedman, *Small Victories*

Jackie hands me her notebook one Thursday. I stay after school to read the eight short entries she's written over the past month.

1. Anthony knows my man from before, Derrick. We don't talk about it though and he's all business these days, reading business. Anyway, Derrick don't come around much. The weather is bad. It's better staying in this Group home than living on the street. Remember those mornings they'd kick me out of the parks and I had to spend my quarter at McDonalds. It was my last quarter and I had no cigarettes. Then I met Derrick.

2. When my mother didn't believe my story about Sam and the nights he came into my room I could hear a door opening in the hallway at the front of the house. The dishes looked too bright all on the counter in the sun. I stopped breathing. And then she dropped the glass.

3. This is about a girl who had only one dress. Her daddy beat her every night. She liked bananas though.

4. They say to write every day. Some days you have your period and the cramps are bad. I'm worried about the spring when Derrick will come around more. My girlfriends told me. He understands about the fight. And he ain't even mad at me for leavin.

5. Anthony is makin it. Landsman can be cold sometimes, makin him start over that week. But now he's makin it. Glad it ain't me. I need my Fridays off. Need to see some of my old friends. I stay out too late on Thursdays. The home is gettin ready to kick me out. I hope they don't. But I like being out late. All my friends are there.

6. If I could write my mom the truth I'd write about the way I almost died when she wouldn't believe me. I'd write about how I stopped breathing.

7. It shits that we have to change into shorts for gym class. My legs are too fat on top. I don't want no one to see my legs all the way up.

8. Once a man pushed me out of his red pickup truck after I gave him a blow job. (I hope it's all right to say blow job, and cocksuckin school in this notebook like I already done). He thought he'd get more. But he only paid ten dollars. So he pushed me out while the truck was moving. I was scabbed up for two weeks and couldn't earn no money. One whole side of my face was scraped. Derrick got mad at me. Those were the best two weeks of all—no work. But no cigarettes either and only a little food.

I write back to Jackie:

I hope you can make it in the group home. I liked Sarah when I met her, and she likes you.

I hated changing for gym. I had to wear little short dresses and white blouses.

After reading your description of the man in the truck, it really makes me hope you'll stay where you are. I worry about your safety, Jackie, and about Derrick.

I'm sorry about your mom and that she didn't believe you. I believe you. Please keep writing.

This darkest part of March is the tough time, the long haul until spring vacation. I am told I have to give the kids a General Information test.

"What is the Wailing Wall?"

Answer: "I can't remember if it is on the left- or the right-hand side of the ship."

"What is the Star of David?"

Answer: "I think it's Charleton Heston."

One Friday, I take the young women to a Mexican restaurant for lunch. I promise them this outing partly to get Jackie into school on a Friday, and, selfishly, because I feel the need to get out of the building.

Mary joins us. I think she feels guilty because she hasn't come to many of the women's group meetings, although in the initial planning she had said she would be there. The girls are quiet on the way over, except for Sandy and Linda laughing in the back of the car. Jackie, up front with me, changes stations on the radio, turning the volume up loud. She chews gum and cracks it the whole ride, drums her fingers, bounces in the seat, rocks back and forth, sings the words to the songs.

Finally we are seated around a table. All the girls except Sandy have gone to the bathroom, stayed ten minutes, and come back smelling of smoke. They are relaxed, drinking Cokes, waiting for tacos.

Sandy still seems removed in her own way, dressed formally in a white silk blouse and long black skirt. Yet she laughs at the jokes, her back curving a little against the chair. It is Sandy who spots Derrick first.

"Hey girl," she says to Jackie. "That man out there wants you." She says it exactly the same way Jackie had yelled those words out of the car window during our drive back from TAMS on the first trip, the day I felt so embarrassed.

We look over at the door, where a tall young man in a long coat is standing, signaling to Jackie. Jackie shakes her head at him. He doesn't move, simply leans back against the door.

"You tell him you were comin' here?" asks Carol.

Jackie shrugs. She ducks her head and her hair drops down, concealing her expression. The veins along her white neck bulge. She won't look at me.

"He ain't leavin'," says Sandy. "Landsman, you go on over there and tell him this is our women's lunch. Ain't no men allowed."

"I'll go," says Jackie, jumping up. Her face is stony, expressionless. Before Mary or I can stop her, she moves to the door and opens it. We cannot hear what they are saying, only see his finger jabbing the air close to her face. Her hands are on her hips.

The girls at the table are silent, eating their food, hunching their shoulders. Mary and I walk outside to confront Derrick. I put my hand on Jackie's arm.

"Your food's gettin' cold," I say. Mary stands flat-footed, glaring at Derrick.

"You get on outta here now. You leave this girl alone, you hear?" Her voice is loud. He smiles at her, salutes her, and turns away.

"Yeah, Mama." He looks at Jackie, who has not turned to come in but stares at him. "I'll catch you later, girl," he says softly. The anger is suddenly gone. He sounds sweet, concerned. He has changed his look completely, become an appealing young boy, a handsome kid. He is charming. Jackie stands immobile, staring at him.

"Come on now, girl, come on in and eat your food," says Mary. She touches Jackie's arm. Jackie pushes by both of us and walks back to her place at the table.

"Why you tell him where you'd be?" asks Sandy. "That was stupid, girl. Ruined your lunch."

"Shut up! Just shut the fuck up," Jackie's voice is loud. An old couple seated two tables away stares at our group.

"What you starin' at? Old farts!" Jackie yells at them. The rest of the girls laugh nervously.

"Okay, okay. Just cool it," Mary and I say at the same time.

Jackie eats her taco in fast, large bites, then stands up.

"You ready to go yet?" she asks. The rest of the girls are still eating.

"Not yet. We're not quite finished," I say. Jackie pushes back her chair until it falls on the floor. She walks away from it and heads to the bathroom. Once she is gone, Carol says, "Ooooh, she's in some deep shit with him."

"Maybe not," I say. "Maybe she's figuring out what to do."

"Maybe," says Sandy, finishing up her Coke. "I don't know, though, Landsman." She shakes her head. I pay the bill, apologizing to the owner for the disruption. He shakes his head, smiles a worn smile.

"Kids. They got some mouths."

I go into the bathroom to find Jackie. She is sitting on the floor of one of the two stalls, the door open. She is smoking.

"We're ready to go," I say.

"That was Derrick," she says, pulling on her Marlboro, letting the smoke out in a smooth stream.

"I guessed." I lean against the side of the stall.

"I shouldn't have told him."

"No. You shouldn't." I don't ask her why she told Derrick we would be here. I learned in one of the many classes I took in education, that the question "why" implies judgment and shuts down kids.

"I thought it would be funny."

"But it wasn't," I say. "He seemed angry."

"He's always angry, Landsman."

"Why?" I ask, forgetting the rule. Jackie shrugs. She drops the rest of her cigarette into the toilet and flushes it down.

The kids are silent on the return trip to school. Jackie sits in back, keeps herself turned toward the window. The kids thank me quickly when we get to the building and head off to their classes. Mary and I walk slowly up the steps.

Mary shakes her head. "That girl is in some big trouble," she says.

I nod. We part at the top of the landing. "Thanks for coming," I say to her as she heads down the hall. She waves wearily.

That afternoon after school is over, Frankie wanders in. He still has no socks. He puts the reading papers I brought to his father on my desk. They are wrinkled and well worn.

"My dad said to give you these. He done with them."

"Thanks, Frankie. Would he like the next set? He could help you with those words with 'i' in them, the new ones."

"Naw. He back in prison." Frankie looks at me.

"I'm sorry to hear that," I say, looking directly back at Frankie. "Maybe when you visit him you could take him some more lists."

Frankie shakes his head. "I don't go visitin' him much," he says. "My uncle just tell me to stay away from him."

I don't know what to say. Frankie squats in front of the bookshelves, then takes out a book on Kareem Abdul Jabar.

"My man, Kareem," he says, to no one. "That my man, Kareem."

Two weeks from spring break, the kids are halfheartedly working in their folders. A young, well-dressed man stands at the door of my first hour class. I don't recognize him.

"Can I speak to Robert for a moment, please?" he asks.

Before I can ask him to come back at the end of the hour, Robert is out of his chair. He picks up a stapler from my desk.

"Get out of the way, Landsman."

I do not move but the stranger does. He slips behind me. I can hear the sound of a switchblade opening.

Robert says, "Come on, fucker, jus' come on!"

Jackie mutters, "Oh, fuck," under her breath.

Robert and the stranger are facing each other, the stranger's knife throwing changing light on the walls of my classroom.

I walk over to Jackie and hand her a book, telling her to bring it to the principal. She looks at me as if I'm crazy but leaves with the book.

Behind me I can hear Robert, "Come on, mother, jus' try to cut, man, jus' try."

I tell the kids to get up and walk quietly out of the room. They don't argue.

Robert and the visitor move around each other in circles.

The principal comes quickly into the room. He is a large man, calm and firm.

"Put the knife away," he says quietly.

"No way, man." That awful light dances in the room as the young man waves the slim blade.

"I said, drop the knife! Robert, take off. Now!" the principal yells at Robert, turning to face him.

Robert stares at the other young man for a minute. Then he moves toward the door. The other kid drops the knife. I pick it up. I can feel the body warmth on the handle. I can feel the sweat on it. The principal reaches out to take the kid by the arm. And then suddenly Robert is back in the room. With amazing speed and strength he pushes the kid out of the principal's range and swings at his face.

I am still holding the knife. I can hear the smack of Robert's fist as it lands on the cheek of the other young man. The sound is repeated, only this time it is Robert's face that shows a dark welt. The principal moves between them. I run to get help. My kids are huddled by the doorway, watching the action. When Ted Marvin sees my face, he is out from behind his desk and running for my classroom. By the time I get there, the two men have separated Robert and the stranger. They take Robert to the office and the other young man to a small room at the end of the hall.

I signal the kids to come back into class with me. I am still holding the knife. My hand is trembling. When I move it, light moves across Johnny's face. I fold the blade into the handle and thrust it into my front desk drawer.

"That his old girlfriend's man," says Mitchell.

"What?" I ask.

"That's the man what goes with Robert's old lady now," says Jackie.

"Why they fightin'? Robert don't even go with her no more," asks Johnny.

"They fight over the kid," says Mitchell. "Robert wants his kid, and his old girlfriend don't want him to have her."

"He should just settle that with her!" says Johnny, " 'stead of bringin' knives and shit to school."

"I agree," I say, wanting to cheer.

The kids are subdued. Jackie chews gum. Mitchell leans his head on his arm. Johnny sucks his thumb.

I know from their stories that these kids have seen more knives than I ever have. I have heard kids say that every time a knife comes out, their palms sweat, an electric current runs up their spines. It does not matter that they have seen all this before. They are anxious each time a car pulls up beside them at the curb.

I look at Johnny. His pants have perfect, paper-thin creases. Jackie's hair is clean; she wears pearl earrings different from the earrings she wore yesterday. This morning I find these students remarkable. I find them amazing: the way they walk into my room, open their books, write lists of spelling words. I silently congratulate them on their arrival in my class, taking up pencils, struggling with prefixes and suffixes.

Robert is suspended for four days. The police come and ask questions. They take the knife. The other young man is to be charged with assault. When Robert comes back, he heads for his old seat by the window. He never mentions the fight. No one else brings it up.

The days move slowly. And the snow won't quit. Linda's father has been sent to prison. He writes her letters, though. She reads them and cries. Carol has become a nomad. She drifts in about once a week and gives us her sweet smile.

I arrange to have Tina, an ex-prostitute, come in to talk to the young women's group. Jackie doesn't want to attend, says she won't be there, that she'd rather not hear about it. She says she doesn't need to hear about what she already knows. I urge her to come anyway. When Tina arrives, Jackie is nowhere to be found. Sandy says she doesn't want the group to start unless Jackie is part of it.

"Then go get her," I say, gambling. "You know where she is."

Linda and Sandy look at each other. They shrug their shoulders and get up. I give them pink hall passes. Under "destination," I write: "To find Jackie and bring her back to 207." Tina and I talk. I am nervous, unsure about whether the two of them will skip out or come back without Jackie. Soon, from the other end of the hall, I hear Jackie's voice.

"Let me go, bitches. I don't need to hear no fuckin' prostitute." She spits out each syllable.

Doors fly open as the other classes watch. Sandy is on Jackie's left side and Linda on the right, pulling her down the hall. She is struggling. I know the strength in Jackie. I know that she could actually get free. There is a look in her eye that is not entirely without pleasure.

By the time she settles down and Tina begins talking, I see that Jackie is frightened.

After her talk and a short movie on the death of a young prostitute, Tina asks for questions.

"Why you quit?" asks Sandy.

"My man started beating on my baby, my two-year-old," she says. "I turned him in."

"He in jail now?" asks Carol, who heard that Tina was coming and dropped in.

"He got out a month ago. That's why I carry a gun in my purse." Tina points to her bulging black purse. "He slashed my tires last week."

"You afraid?" asks Linda.

"Yeah."

Jackie has been silent the whole time, her head down. Now she looks up.

"Why you get started?" she asks.

"My friend introduced me to my pimp," she says. "He was my boyfriend for awhile. Then he put me out."

"You like it?" Jackie stares at Tina.

"For a few months. I liked drugs, too."

"Then what happened after a few months?" Sandy asks this, anticipating what Jackie wants to know.

"I got tired of the johns, of the diseases I got from them. When I stopped doing drugs, I didn't need my man no more."

"Then he beat your baby?"

"Yeah."

"So, how'd you quit?" asks Carol.

"First time, I ran away to North Dakota for six months. But he just waited till I came back. And I went with him again because it was winter, and I was gettin' cold."

The girls laugh.

"The second time I left for good. Went to the cop station. Went to see some cop I knew. Took my little girl right into the station. She was beat up. I was beat up."

"You ever want to go back?" I ask. My voice startles the girls. I think they had forgotten that I was in the room.

"Yeah. When I'm hungry. Now I got this job," she says.

"You still got your little girl?" asks Linda.

"Oh, yeah." Tina smiles, showing bad teeth. "My mom takes her most days when I work. She live with me, though."

Tina gets up and begins rewinding the film. No one has much to say; they are just waiting for the bell to ring. Jackie walks over to the window, opens it, and yells out to the kids picking up bats and balls on the playing field, "Hey, you! You're cute!" Her voice is unusually loud.

I walk over to her and pull the window closed.

"Fuck this shit!" she says and walks out of the room, slamming the door.

I don't chase her. The bell will ring in a minute. I let her go. After class Sandy stays behind.

"Jackie didn't fight us so hard, you know."

"I know. Thanks for getting her."

"She's doin' okay," says Sandy.

"Yeah."

"My aunt Rhonda say she needs some healin'," says Sandy.

"She does need that," I say.

During the summer I was raped, I spent some time in Woodbridge, my hometown. I didn't tell many people about the rape. Somewhere inside me I still wondered whether it was my fault. I needed someone I could call in the middle of the night when I couldn't sleep, afraid to smoke in my parents' house. One afternoon I told Marty Stephens, my closest friend in grade school and junior high. We saw each other every summer of my boarding school and college years. When I blurted the story out in their pine-paneled recreation room, rich with deep carpeting, leather furniture, and a fully stocked bar, there was an abrupt silence. Marty slid down further into her brown leather chair. I changed the subject quickly and talked about things we both loved: clothes, horses, her father's good looks. I left that room as soon as I could, walking down the hill, along the dirt road, through the Stoddards' field.

Marty never called me after that. And I pulled away from her: I didn't wander up the hill to chat with her mother, didn't suggest we swim together at one of our neighbors' houses.

Fifteen years later, Marty apologized to me for her reaction.

"I blamed you," she said. "I thought it was your fault. But now I walk around the campus at Palo Alto at night carrying mace and an alarm that can puncture an eardrum." She shifted on her flowered chair, turned toward me, directly. "I keep thinking of you," she said. "I keep thinking of how I blamed you."

We were sitting in her charming living room. Her children were roller-skating on the sidewalk and up and down a ramp they had built themselves. I realized then how much we do to speed healing without even knowing that we do it. I realized that years ago, her silence, her body falling deeper and deeper into that chair, the phone calls she never made—signaled me to stay away from her.

And now, I think that perhaps the kids I teach are doing what they need to do to protect themselves, using blind instinct, trying to heal their hurts.

Yet they seem to be making such awful mistakes. Carol drinks, Linda curls into a ball, Sandy glares from her artificial height, keeping herself separate. And Jackie, in her tight pink pants and white T-shirt, is calling to men, walking down Chicago Avenue at two A.M.

I find it hard to know where or when to step in, how to break a pattern, how to help them change.

The day after Tina's talk is Friday. Jackie surprises me again by showing up for class, since Fridays are usually her "days off." She heads to the other side of the room and opens the window. This time she just leans on the sill, watching the softball game getting started. If she had yelled at the class down there, I would have asked her to leave. Instead she closes the window after a few minutes, sits down at her place, and takes out her notebook. Everyone leaves her alone. She writes for the entire hour, handing the journal to me at the end of class.

"You read it," she says, almost threateningly.

I nod. "You want me to write you something back?"

"Naw. You just read it. I'll know if you've read it. I can tell." She smiles, her face softening around that smile.

"Okay." I smile back.

I take out the notebook after the last bell has rung. She hasn't written for weeks. There is only today's entry:

> *1. My grandmother said I could come live with her. I'm tired of this Group Home. They make you come in when the streets are just getting interesting. So, I'll move out tomorrow or the next day. And then Derrick won't know where I am, neither. I can't figure out why I'm so hyper these days. Maybe it's the dope that Bart gives me. He's my new man. He's twenty-seven years old and my grandmother already says he can't come around her house. That don't matter. We can meet places. We can meet at the lakes when the weather gets warm. I don't care. I just want to stay out a little later at night. Only trouble with my grandmother is she believes in all that Jesus stuff, wants me to go to church with her. She's afraid I will follow the devil.*
>
> *I wish I didn't have to worry about Derrick all the time. He has a fine car. He kept me in cigarettes. For awhile I was his primary woman. But then there was the fight. Right near the co-op food store where the hippies hang out. We were in the middle of it—some gang was after Derrick, and his own gang was helping him out. And there were rocks and boards being thrown and cars screeching their brakes. There were cars jig-jag across the lawns. Someone waved a knife at Derrick. He threw me in front of him but I got away and the knife went into him, right through his white shirt. He screamed and the other man ran away. Later, in the hospital, I told him I was sorry for jumpin out of the way. He didn't mind, he said. But he still looked angry. So I went back to the place, packed up my things, and left. I like the streets. But I don't like that kind of stuff. So. I don't know. He still looks for me.*
>
> *I want Anthony to come back and learn to read again, or maybe Carol to come and talk about herself. It's getting to be spring. My mom hasn't written back but my grandma said she probably would write soon. I don't know what she'll say. It doesn't matter so much. I got Bart. He's coming over to help me move. I don't know what my grandmother will say but I*

need help getting my stuff out of the home. She better not fight me over this. I'm tired of people fighting me.

Later that day I talk to Jane about Jackie's situation. She calls the group home, trying to keep Jackie from leaving. I sit in her office, take the phone, and tell Sarah I think it will be a mistake for Jackie to move out. Sarah says that she knows this but that they've given Jackie four chances already, and she continues to keep violating curfew. There's a waiting list for her place, and they can't let the other girls see her get away with repeated violations of their rules.

Jane sighs as she puts down the phone. We look at each other. The next class has begun, and I've got to get upstairs to the kids.

"Maybe it'll work with the grandmother," Jane says.

"Yeah. Maybe."

The day before spring vacation the girls are sitting in my room, talking and eating chips and dip. Outside, that cold March rain that bites into the bones is coming down steadily. Karen is back. However, Davey is not. Karen says he's making lots of money now that he's gone to California.

Jackie is talking about a horror movie she saw on television.

"Don't you hate it after those movies, when you start to hear noises, when the house starts movin'?" asks Carol.

"Yeah. And you're all alone down in the basement, and you don't want to go upstairs 'cause you sure somebody's there?"

"Yeah," says Sandy.

"Your aunt let you watch movies on TV?" asks Jackie.

"She don't let me, I just do it," says Sandy.

"Oooooh, she tough!" says Karen, rolling her eyes.

Everyone laughs, including Sandy.

"Hey, girl, you gotta nice ol' smile," Jackie says, looking at Sandy. "Why don't you smile like that more often. You might get a fine young man that way."

Sandy looks at the table, then at the ceiling.

"We were talking about scary shows, not boys," says Karen, picking at a scab on her wrist.

"I just sleep in the basement some nights. Leave the ol' TV on," says Jackie. She is in a good mood today.

"I never got to watch TV late," I say.

"Your mama stricter than Sandy's aunt?" Carol asks, incredulous. "No one could be stricter than that."

"I went to boarding school," I say.

"So? Didn't they have no TVs in boarding school?"

"Yeah. But we had to be in our rooms by nine-thirty and lights out by ten o'clock."

"Couldn't you sneak out and watch it?" asked Jackie. "I mean after people were in bed?"

"No, they patrolled the halls."

"What you eat there?" she asks.

"Good food. Homemade bread, meat, vegetables."

"Any munchies?"

"Sometimes. You couldn't have much of your own food in your room, though."

"You get any weekend passes?"

"Nope. I stayed there on the weekends."

"What you do there?"

"Study hall in the morning on Saturdays. Gym class in the afternoon. Church on Sunday."

"Man, I don't care how good the food is, it sounds cold to me," says Karen.

"Sounds like my man's time at the County Home Reform School!" says Carol, laughing.

"Sounds worse than County Home!" says Jackie. "They get to watch TV late there."

"They get weekend passes sometimes."

"So why you go to that school?" asks Jackie.

I shift in my chair. I am not used to having the attention focused on me like this.

"My mother went there. My parents thought it was the best place for me to get an education."

"You think so?" asks Sandy.

"I don't know. I learned how to study there. I learned how to eat fancy meals with lots of silverware."

"You learn to sew—you know, in one of those circle things on your lap?" asks Linda. Her voice is quiet, shy. She hasn't spoken all hour.

I laugh. "Embroidery? No."

"So, didn't you miss your mom?" asks Jackie.

"Yeah. I missed her, and I missed just being at home, watching TV, staying up late, and wearing my own clothes."

"Whose clothes you wear, then?" asks Sandy. The girls giggle.

"Uniforms. Green jumpers. White blouses. High socks. Brown shoes."

"Every day? Like in them Catholic schools?"

"Yep."

"To bed?" They giggle again.

"No. I was allowed to wear my own pajamas."

"Oooooh," they say, whistling, sounding sexy. "Your own pajamas!"

"Hey! We were talking about horror movies," says Karen again.

"Oh, yeah."

"You get to watch *any* TV in your boarding school?" asks Jackie. She has been looking at me intently all hour.

"Nope. None, really. Maybe once in a while on a Saturday morning."

"What your house like?" asks Jackie.

"I thought we were talking about horror movies," says Karen again.

"Shut up! Landsman's telling us a horror movie about her boarding school."

"My house was beautiful," I say. "I had a bedroom with my sister, and it was out away from the city."

"Oh." Jackie sounds almost disappointed. "You like your mom?"

"Yeah. I did. Sometimes she got upset with me."

"What for?"

"Probably stayed out all night, huh?"

"Once or twice. Later. When I was in college and she found out."

"What else she get upset about?" asks Jackie.

"When I got moody, you know, when I didn't want to talk to anyone. Then I'd kind of sulk, I guess."

"Your mom hit you?" asks Sandy.

"No. She never hit me."

"Your dad?"

"Only twice. We got spankings, but hardly ever."

"This ain't no horror story!" says Karen.

They clean up the chips and dip, brush off the table with the paper towels I brought from the bathroom to use as napkins.

When the bell rings, Jackie stays behind by my desk.

"How many bathrooms in your house, Landsman?"

"Three," I say.

Jackie rolls her eyes. She gets out some gum, offers me a piece. "Three bathrooms. Holy shit." She walks out, letting the wrapper flutter to the floor.

Over the week-long spring break, I sleep late, drink a second cup of coffee, and read the newspaper slowly and carefully.

When I am in the supermarket one afternoon, Johnny Washington runs up to me.

"You're shopping!" he says, amazed.

"Yep." I smile.

"You're buyin' bread!"

"Yep, I am."

He watches as I walk through the check-out line. I turn and wave. He's staring at me and my bag of groceries.

APRIL

*"Eleven years from now they will become the men
and women of Flint or Paradise, the majors of a
minor town, and I will be gone into smoke or
memory, so I bow to them here and whisper
all I know, all I will ever know."*

—Philip Levine, "Among Children,"
What Work Is

I am not eager to return after vacation. The end of the school year is tough for me, as well as for the kids. As the weather gets warmer, they become restless, inattentive, hard to keep at work. I think of a garden I'd like to start, the garden I plan almost every year and rarely get around to putting in. I daydream, pace the room, run out of new ideas.

Jackie has spent this vacation with her grandmother.

"I seen the devil," she tells me on Monday morning, first thing. "I seen him."

"You did?" asks Sandy. She moves away from Jackie and carefully straightens her flowered shirt.

"In my closet. There was a picture of Jesus Christ. I heard someone cryin' in that closet at night. Next morning I go in and there's holes all over Jesus's face."

"Lord, girl, I don't want to hear this," says Sandy, putting her hands over her ears.

"Well, I'm fightin' the devil. I am. But sometimes I don't know if I'll win," says Jackie, looking at her long purple fingernails.

Sandy picks up her books and moves to the other side of the room from Jackie. This is the first time this year that she has sat in a different chair. Johnny's eyes are wide. He stopped reading his book and has been listening. Later, I know he'll come up to me and ask about the devil. Just a week ago he wanted to know if the eclipse was going to be the end of the world.

Mitchell just shakes his head. He continues to fill out answers on a word puzzle sheet.

"I mean it," says Jackie to no one in particular. Her green blouse glitters in the morning light that falls across her shoulders. Today she wears clothes that look like neon, as though somewhere behind the material is an electric switch.

"I been goin' to church with my grandmother. But I find myself wrestling with the devil all the while I'm setting there," she says. "I mean, he is sayin' to me to jump up, to call out, right there in the middle of that church."

"Girl, you just stop your talkin'," says Sandy. "How we 'sposed to get this readin' done with you talkin'?" She turns away from the class, staring down at her book.

Jackie is still talking, has not even heard Sandy.

"Sometimes I want to kill my stepbrother," says Jackie. "I remember him comin' into my room and yellin' about something. The devil tells me to go ahead and try to kill him with a knife."

"Landsman, I can't hear no more of this shit," says Johnny. I move close to him and rest my hand on his shoulder until he goes back to reading his book.

Jackie looks around her. Everyone has turned away. They're all doing their "ignoring job," as I call it. She puts another piece of gum in her mouth. She wears six different rings on two fingers. I sit down next to her and put my arm around her shoulder. I rarely come this close. She does not flinch or shrug or push me off. She simply bows her head a moment and then quietly opens her folder. I stay beside her for five minutes, looking through the picture book of dogs she keeps near her during the time she is in my room.

The room is quiet. I rarely get such silence. Even Johnny is enjoying the easy reading books I've found. I always bring the book I'm reading to school, in case there are moments like these.

For fifteen minutes we hear only the sounds of the class outside on the field or a car honking on the street.

Breaking the quiet, Sandy asks, "You married in the spring, Landsman?"

I look up, startled. "No, in the fall. And then in the winter."

"What?"

"I had two weddings. One Christian, for my parents. One Jewish, for Maury's parents."

"So, how do you get divorced?" asks Jackie. She has been staring out the window for ten minutes, ignoring the article open on the table in front of her.

"Guess I don't," I say.

She shrugs, gets out another stick of gum. We have another quiet period until the bell rings.

Sandy stops by my desk to ask, "Can I bring my niece to school?"

Sandy's been having a good year and we need a diversion.

"If Rhonda can come pick her up after first hour. Fine." I smile.

Sandy smiles back.

Jasmine is beautiful. She is everything that Sandy has said she is. We sit and stare at her, fascinated. She smiles for us all, but especially for Johnny. I wonder if she likes Johnny because he is so short, closer to her size.

Sandy passes her to Robert. He holds Jasmine with a surprising amount of ease. I keep forgetting that he has a daughter, now three years old. Watching him here, with Jasmine on his knee, chuckling as he bounces her up and down, I am reminded of Robert's fatherhood, of how quickly lives change. Mitchell doesn't pay much attention to Sandy or the baby. He's got seven brothers and sisters at home and isn't interested.

When Jackie reaches her purple fingernails toward Jasmine, Sandy snatches the baby away.

"No way! You aren't touchin' my baby girl." Sandy's anger is mixed with terror. "Don't want no devil girl holdin' my baby!" Jackie shrugs her shoulders, picks up a pencil, and twirls it in her fingers.

Then Sandy sets Jasmine on my lap. She is a fat baby, dressed in a frilly blue dress, tiny socks, and white Mary Jane shoes with gold buckles. The kids all watch as I play with her, as she smiles. They gather around me as they do on those days I read to them from books. Even Robert joins the group.

"You wish you had a little one again, Landsman?" asks Johnny.

"Yeah. I'd like to have a baby around."

"How old were you when you had your boy?" asks Sandy.

"Twenty-four."

No one says anything for a few minutes.

Jackie has not offered to hold the baby again. From across the room she says, "Landsman did it right. Shouldn't have no babies 'til you're ready."

"You sayin' there's something wrong with this here little girl?" asks Sandy, straightening her shoulders, looking down from her angry height.

"No, girl. Shit! I didn't say there was nothin' wrong with her! She's cute."

Jackie sounds weary now. She shakes her head, leans on the sill.

"My mom had me when she was seventeen," says Johnny.

"Mine was eighteen," says Mitchell.

"And you both turned out fine," I say.

"Yeah," says Johnny. "Turned out just fine." He picks a piece of lint off his pants, stands up, and twirls around.

Jackie smiles. She walks over to Johnny and straightens his collar. He looks up at her and then ducks his head.

"Don't mess with my clothes, girl," he says, grinning.

"Yeah," Jackie says, stepping back, one hand on her hip. "You turned out fine-little, but just fine."

A few moments before the final bell rings, Rhonda comes into the room. She walks over to Sandy, who is holding Jasmine's hands and standing the baby up on her lap. Then Rhonda turns back to look at me.

"Was it all right?" she asks.

"Fine," I say. "This was a nice break for all of us. She's beautiful."

"Yes. She's beautiful," says Rhonda.

I walk out into the hall with Rhonda and Jasmine.

"How are you doing?" I ask. "I haven't heard from you in a while."

"I'm fine. Jus' fine. Sandy's settled down and that helps. She's really trying to read faster now."

"Good," I say. "That's the next step."

"Well, thank you for all you've done this year," says Rhonda. "Between you and the Good Lord, things seem better."

Rhonda waves Jasmine's tiny hand in my direction. The bell rings and kids immediately surround her. She continues to walk slowly while they dance and run by her, grabbing for each other behind her back. At the end of the corridor, Rhonda turns and looks in my direction. She waves her long brown arm up over the kids tumbling by. I wave back. Rhonda is only twenty-seven, already a mother and a grandmother.

My sister Lesley calls from Indiana to break the news that Walter has cancer. She herself is heavy on her feet, a month from delivery. Her daughter Carey is having tantrums, and Walter is curled up on a hospital bed in Indianapolis, one hundred miles away, waiting for her to come and drive him home.

I find it difficult to know what to say to comfort her. I send her notes, tell her I'll fly in whenever she needs me the most.

The next day at the end of first hour, I ask the kids about where they've lived. Johnny says his favorite house was one near Lake Street and Thirty-seventh.

"Why'd you like that house so much?" asks Jackie.

"Cause we played so many games there," he says. "We ran around the neighborhood, anywhere we wanted to go."

"That's always the way it is, wherever you live when you're little," says Mitchell. "You always like that house 'cause you had no school then."

"I hear that," says Robert, smiling.

"I liked school," says Jackie. Then, while the rest of the kids are groaning, she adds under her breath, "I hated home."

Sandy hears her say it. But instead of her usual, "What you mean girl, you hated home?" she lets it go. She looks at me.

Later that day, during the women's group meeting, Sandy says in a voice that is quieter than usual, "Why you hate home?" She is looking at Jackie.

Since Jackie has stopped talking about the devil as abruptly as she started, Sandy is beginning to warm up to her again.

" 'Cause I was scared of my stepbrother. The things he did to me." Jackie snaps her gum nervously after she says this.

Karen has dropped back into the group for a while. "Yeah. My mama's boyfriend is like that."

Again, there's silence. Then Jackie says in an unusually loud voice, "But, fuck, man, now I got me a man that can protect me."

"What? Some new pimp?" asks Karen. "I don't need no pimp."

"You just earn money showin' yourself in the movies!" shouts Jackie. "You work for pimps, girl."

"Look. No bad-mouthing each other in this group," I interrupt.

They settle back, sullen.

Before I can jump in with soothing or encouraging words, Carol speaks up.

"Man. That must be dog. Always worryin' about someone in your own house comin' after you." There is such complete sympathy in her voice, as she moves her head back and forth, such empathy even as she imagines it, that no one else says anything for a moment.

I can still smell their perfume after they have left the room. I arrange to see the social worker again to talk about Karen. The next class will be here in a minute. I pick up Sharon's gum wrapper and toss it in the wastebasket.

That afternoon I take my usual three-and-a-half mile run along the river. The weather is warm enough that I can wear shorts. My legs look white and unhealthy to me. I feel fat, winter-layered. My breathing comes easily, though, and I don't get a side stitch. Maybe I'll run a ten-kilometer women's race in June.

When Maury comes home, I describe the girls' group session, the way Carol sounded, Jackie's anger. I follow him upstairs. He changes into blue jeans and a T-shirt, barely looking at me. When he speaks, it is about putting the air conditioners back in the upstairs windows. Aaron comes home and rummages around in the kitchen. By the time we get downstairs, he has earphones on, nodding his head to The Clash.

I wanted Maury to tell me how sorry he felt about Jackie. I wanted him to ask me what I think about whether she'll make it.

He reaches under the counter for a vegetable steamer. These are my kids,

I want to tell him. Listen to what has happened to them. We eat dinner. The boys across the street are throwing a softball instead of a football.

After the dishes are washed, Maury goes upstairs to the study to watch television. Aaron settles in to talk on the phone. I curl up next to Maury on the couch and fall asleep there at eight-thirty in the evening.

The next day one of the nomads returns to my classroom. Last year when Jimmy Shadow came to my room, he was mistaken for a girl because he was so pretty. He has light brown skin. His hair is soft and curls around his face. His brown eyes are round with long, thick lashes, and his smile reveals perfect teeth. He is slim, usually dressed in jeans, an old T-shirt, and a jean jacket.

Bill, the man who worked as a group leader in our program, stopped by my room. He asked me, indicating Jimmy, "Do you want to show her where breakfast is served?"

"Who you mean, *her!*" Jimmy asked, pushing his thin body up and out of the chair.

"Sorry," Bill said.

At that point neither of us knew that Jimmy's father was black, his mother Native American. Nor did we know that Jimmy was living with his father because his mother had come out as a lesbian. At fourteen, Jimmy didn't want to be around his mom and her lover.

Jimmy was terrified of reading. He had defeated the most patient teachers, waited them out, and finally convinced them that he could never learn. The first day of class I sat across from him, showing him my photograph book of dogs. I asked him to talk about the kinds of animals he loved, and he talked about the pit bulls, the German shepherds, the dogs that wandered in the alleys behind his mother's house. After that day, I took him for walks after school. Slowly he came to talk about his mother, his father, which side of town he was living on at the time. He changed homes almost every month—moved back with his mother and her lover, then in with his father again.

One spring morning, his dad accompanied Jimmy to meet with the staff. His father said that Jimmy was going through a difficult time because Jimmy was not sure whether he was gay or straight, boy or girl, black or Native American. Jimmy began to cry silently. He would not meet our eyes. And all we could say, all we could ever say to these kids, or their parents, was that we would be there when they needed to talk.

This past September, against our wishes but with the permission of his father, Jimmy registered at South Central High School, determined to make it in a regular school.

A friend of mine who teaches at South Central said she saw Jimmy walking the halls all day, unwilling to go into his classes. Now he was back, defeated.

I wonder about whether it is wise to bring him into my room at this point in the year. I am not sure I have the patience.

"Oh, no," says Johnny, when he sees Jimmy. "Not him." Johnny remembers Jimmy's anger, his tantrums from the year before.

"What's wrong with him? He's cute," says Jackie, smiling at Jimmy.

Jimmy smiles back. I am struck again, as I was when I first met him, by the physical beauty of this young man.

"Jimmy, I'm glad you're back," I say.

But Jimmy knows I'm not so sure. He knows that by late April, my patience runs thin. He does not know, none of them know, that I am preoccupied with my sister Lesley and her husband's bout with cancer. Yet some of the kids can tell I am distracted. I cannot figure out why I haven't mentioned it to them. Perhaps I am demanding the same thing for myself that I demand for the kids: the right not to tell.

"So. How's it goin?" Jackie asks Jimmy.

"So. Okay," he answers, shrugging his shoulders. Again, I am not surprised that they know each other: many of these kids help each other find places to sleep, lend each other money. Jimmy did drugs last year, came in some mornings with blurred speech, slurring his words.

"You still hangin' out with the crowd? Derrick around?" asks Jimmy.

"Nope," Jackie answers. "I don't see him no more."

Jimmy shrugs his shoulders again and approaches my desk.

"So, Landsman, you still got them dumb cards?"

"Yeah. I still have your old folder, too." I pull it out of my file cabinet. Having worked with nomads as long as I have, I've learned never to throw anything away for at least two years.

Jimmy looks amused. He opens the folder and begins reading a list of words: "ake: bake, cake, make, take, sake . . ."

He shakes his head and closes the folder.

"I don't want to do that crap. I already been in South Central High School."

"But you're here now, Jimmy. Let's work on your reading so you can go back to South next spring."

"Forget that," says Jimmy and throws a pencil across the room. He begins throwing everything from my desk across the room.

"See, Landsman!" Johnny says and puts his head down on the desk.

"Oh, he's a bad little dude," says Jackie, smiling.

"Yeah, I am," Jimmy says.

Sandy has not moved. Jackie starts laughing. Robert tells them to shut up, and Mitchell walks out of the room.

Mitchell doesn't know that there's a new aide out in the hall. He comes back immediately, his eyes huge.

"Shit, man, I'm stayin' in here."

Curt, the aide, walks in right after him. Curt is 6'5" tall and weighs about 250 pounds. He's Native American and an ex-con. And he's smiling.

"This young gentleman here didn't seem to know that he leaves when the bell rings. Seems he thought it was time to leave already."

"Thanks," I say.

Curt leaves.

"Who the fuck is that?" asks Jimmy.

"He's our new administrative aide."

"Shit!" says Johnny.

Jimmy stands up, sticking out his chest.

"Don't matter to me. I've run away from bigger guys."

When the bell rings, instead of the usual mad dash for the door, the kids stop and peer cautiously up and down the hall. Curt is standing at one end, smiling.

I stop and talk to Jane to catch up on what is happening with Jimmy. I find out that he's living with his mother at the moment and that his father sees him on weekends. At South Central, he tried classes but because he couldn't read the textbooks, he skipped. He'd drop in, run around the building, yell into other classes, and run out again. They suspended him three times and finally called downtown; after a placement conference, he was readmitted to our program.

"He must feel like a total failure," I say, taking out the apple I have brought into her room.

"Yeah. I guess. But I did talk to his special ed teacher, who thinks he may be ready for a breakthrough. She said he really tried his reading with her whenever he dropped into school. She says she thinks that you got the idea of phonics into his head."

I shrug. "I don't know," I say. "I don't know if we'll ever get to reading. He's not settling down at all."

"Let's wait and see. How does Jackie seem, by the way?"

"Jackie. Tenuous. I'm not sure about this move in with her grandmother. She came into class, talked about the devil and church and scared Sandy and the other kids."

Jane nods. "Mrs. Blakesley is very religious. May be a problem. Might not. We'll just hope."

I throw the apple core in her basket and pluck a caramel out of the jar she keeps for the kids.

A student knocks on Jane's door. This young man looks about thirteen and is in obvious distress.

"Take care," says Jane, as I leave.

"You too," I say, heading for class.

A few days later, a psychiatrist stops in during my free hour to see me about Jimmy. He has come from the university with forms to fill out and plans to raise his self-esteem. He is a precise young man who holds his pencil gracefully. My room is disheveled, one chair leaning precariously against the wall, books and papers strewn on the floor.

He asks how he should talk to Jimmy. Staring past him for a moment, at the squirrel on a branch near my window, I say, "Don't ask him about his family."

The man shrugs, tightens his thin wool tie. He smiles at me. "Oh?" he says, raising his blond eyebrows.

"Yeah," I answer. "If he trusts you, maybe in a month or so he'll tell you."

"He's a mixed kid, isn't he?" he asks earnestly.

"Jimmy's mother is Indian and his dad is black. He hates to be reminded."

"Of the father, being black?"

"Not necessarily," I say.

I am tired. I want this man to go away despite the fact that Jimmy needs help from many different sources.

"We'll see how it goes," he says. "Just trying to keep Jimmy from dropping out of school. I'll see what I can do."

"Just don't ask personal questions," I repeat.

Later, during fourth hour, I hear a door bang against a wall and the sound of loud voices. No one even looks up. We are used to anger and trust the assistant principal to deal with it. I bend over Frankie, who is beginning to learn two-syllable words. Suddenly my door swings open and Jimmy comes running in, followed by an assistant principal, Sam. I signal to Sam to leave him with me. Jimmy goes over by the window. His face is pale.

"Motherfucker," he mutters under his breath. None of us moves. If Jimmy can just stay here and get himself under control he'll be making progress. He stands, quietly watching the squirrel in the tree outside the window. After a few minutes and many more epithets muttered quietly, Jimmy slumps down into a chair. "That white motherfucker wanted to know about my daddy."

"Don't tell him," says Frankie, looking up from a story he is trying to read. "You don't got to tell him nothin' about your daddy." Frankie goes back to his book.

"I ain't tellin' him nothin' about nothin'," Jimmy says. "Do I got to?" He looks at me.

"No, but maybe you could talk to him about school. About why you can't stay at the high school, about your fights."

"No, he only want to know about my daddy."

I turn back to the class and work with Linda. Jimmy picks up a picture book about dogs. The rest of the hour goes quietly and when the bell rings, he looks carefully out my doorway, runs down the stairs, and takes off, away from the building.

Later, while a group of teachers are eating lunch, the psychiatrist stops by. "Jimmy was not very cooperative."

"He doesn't like personal questions," I repeat, slicing up a block of cheese, setting the square pieces on crackers.

"Honey, you didn't ask that child about his daddy, now did you?" asks Mary, who knows Jimmy and all his relatives.

"He has to confront his background some time," says the young man, tending to the crease in his pants. Mary just shakes her head.

After he leaves, Mary says, "They think they know so much. They don't understand these kids. You've got to step carefully around their home lives. Whew! That gives 'em a fit when you ask 'em stuff about their home lives."

"Remember the guy from the university who wanted to test all our kids' IQs?" asks Ted Marvin.

"Yeah." Jill laughs. "Remember that we told him it wouldn't work, but he came anyway?"

"By the end of the morning the kids had that poor little white guy locking himself in the bathroom, afraid to come out!" Mary chuckles.

We all laugh. It is not laughter born of arrogance. It is just a good feeling to laugh when, once in awhile, you are proven right. So much of what we do seems to rise out of instinct. It's good to remember the times that our knowledge about these kids is borne out.

The psychiatrist, Greg, comes back a week later, but Jimmy has figured out the schedule and stays away. Eventually Greg stops coming. I am not really surprised. Greg refused to acknowledge the insights of those of us who are in the thick of things, who wipe the pencil lead across our foreheads without even knowing it and leave a dark smudge, who talk to the kids every day. This daily knowledge of ours is just what Greg feels he must rise above; he seems to believe that something beyond the gathering of details gives him the authority to ignore the details.

I think about what I have learned. The trick is to respect the details without being swallowed by them.

I think about how Jackie has changed over the year, about Sandy and her willingness now to read aloud from the Bible. I think about all of us here at school who recognize the nervousness in Jimmy's walk. We take in the way a girl leans against a locker. We consider why the letters waver in a child's notebook, the sound of a voice slurring the simplest of words, an earring glinting in a young man's ear. We try to take this knowledge and see where it might fit, to figure out a pattern.

The next morning, Jackie's grandmother arrives at 6:45 A.M. She walks with a cane, is dressed in gray with a clean white sweater over her shoulders. She has requested a conference, and this is the only time she can meet with us, since she works all day at a dry-cleaning store. Her hands are gnarled by arthritis, and her eyes are lined and puffy. She is a combination of toughness and fragility that I've seen often in the kids.

The conference is brief. We are sleepy, and our minds are on our own classes, on who might be waiting at our doors, or on unfinished planning we've interrupted, forgetting that Mrs. Blakesley was coming. Conferences never go as well before school. We are fuzzy-headed and reaching for coffee.

"How is it going with Jackie?" asks Jane. "We are pleased that she is coming to school regularly."

"I don't know." Mrs. Blakesley shakes her head. "She knows what she has to do for me, and she knows she can stay if she does it. Can't say I like her choice of friends very much."

"Is she coming home late?"

"I don't let her," says Mrs. Blakesley, her voice firm. "She knows she can't come home after midnight."

Midnight. That's better than the 10:30 P.M. curfew at the group home.

I find it frustrating that Jackie left that home to gain an extra one-and-a-half hours on the weekends. I remember Sarah's real affection for Jackie. Mrs. Blakesley seems to feel an obligation to Jackie, but I don't hear any warmth.

"Do you think she'll ever go back to her mother?"

"Not until my daughter gets rid of that man and his son." She says this with anger, with barely concealed contempt in her voice.

"So, Jackie will stay with you for a while?"

"As long as she obeys the rules and goes to church on Sundays." Mrs. Blakesley sets her heavy purse down on the table as she says this, as if to emphasize her point. Her hair is wispy in the breeze from the open window. We can hear students calling to each other as they come in. We can hear lockers being opened, books dropping to the floor, exclamations of frustration. We need to be in our classrooms.

"She is really helping Mitchell with his reading. She's a good tutor," I say, hoping to prod Mrs. Blakesley into expressing something other than neutrality toward Jackie.

"She's always been a good little reader." I sense it then, some pride, some nudge of memory. "Used to read out loud all the time when she was little."

I try to imagine Jackie as a little girl. Sometimes I forget that these kids have childhoods, have had good years, easy homes.

"Is there anything we can do here? Any way we can help you?" asks Jane.

"Just make her keep likin' it here, I guess. That's all you can do." Mrs. Blakesley sounds uncertain, resigned to whatever happens. I realize how much is up to Jackie. Mrs. Blakesly pushes back her chair.

"I got to get to work," she says, rising slowly.

"Thank you for stopping by here so early," says Ted Marvin, standing up and holding out his hand.

"I don't know what I can do. Just wanted to meet you all."

"We appreciate that."

"She says this school isn't so bad. That's pretty unusual for her." Mrs. Blakesley smiles for the first time as she looks around at us. Then she walks with difficulty toward the door.

The halls are filled with kids. We wait for an opening in the crowd, and I help Mrs. Blakesley to the stairs, escorting her down to the first floor. I open the heavy metal doors and watch her walk cautiously to the bus stop. She doesn't look back.

Johnny runs into the empty room, out of breath. Sandy walks in wearing a white sundress. She sits demurely off to one side, but she smiles when I compliment her on her clothes. Jackie arrives next, dressed in her jeans and T-shirt. She gives Sandy an appraising look.

"Whoa, girl! You got some pretty clothes. Why you dressed up? You got a man?"

Sandy smiles. "No. Just decided."

"You look *bad*," says Johnny. He is still panting after his run from the basketball court.

They each settle down. Jimmy has been absent from first hour all week, so we have had a quiet time, relieved not to have to watch his every move.

When Jimmy does return he refuses to respond to any of his teachers. Not touch, no coaxing, no praise can get him to settle down. His face is distorted with anger from morning until late afternoon. I am determined to start each day over with him as though the slate is wiped clean.

One morning he comes in and arranges three chairs in a row. He stretches out on them. He puts his head on a book as though it is a pillow, but he does not sleep. He makes animal noises, squawks and squeals. Jackie walks over to his "couch" and squats down close to his head. She pulls the hair back from one side of her face and curls it behind her ear to whisper to him. I cannot hear her words. Then she goes back to her chair and takes out her notebook. Jimmy smiles. Everyone else is working.

For a few minutes Jimmy is quiet. Then suddenly he sits up, rubs his eyes, and looks around. No one responds to him. He pushes the chairs apart and takes the book he was using as a pillow over to the open window. He throws the book out onto the field. I start toward him. He reaches down to the shelf below the window and grabs a pile of sports magazines. He begins throwing them out onto the playing field, one at a time. They flutter down like clumsy birds.

His behavior reaches an anger in me that feels dangerous, as though I'll lose control. Maybe the anger is triggered by the phone call from my sister Lesley the night before, by her exhaustion, and the sound of her four-year-old daughter's voice whining in the background. Maybe it grows out of my sympathy for the other kids exposed to his behavior. None of us should have to put up with such disruption. It's spring and our time to relax.

Finally, I call into the hall to Curt and ask him to take Jimmy out of my classroom, something I rarely do. Jimmy sees Curt coming and begins to back away into a corner, kicking out with his foot, pushing his arms straight into the air.

"Come on, man, out of the room," Curt says quietly.

"Fuck you, man. I mean, just fuck you, you big ol' redskin."

"Hey, Jimmy, man, you're part Indian, so fuck off," says Robert. He has reached his limit.

I ask the kids to ignore what's going on and to work in their folders. I even try the M & M emergency routine. For every two minutes that they ignore Jimmy and Curt, I put an M & M on their desks.

Sandy looks disgusted, as do Johnny and Mitchell as they catch sight of Jimmy out of the corner of their eyes. Jackie freezes. Her face becomes hard. Finally, Curt moves in to restrain Jimmy. Jimmy jumps around him, but Curt manages to grab a shoulder.

"Fuck you, man. You get your drug-addict, prison hands off me!" Jimmy yells.

Curt puts his arms around Jimmy from behind and holds him in a backwards bear hug. Jimmy kicks and Curt holds on. Jimmy spits and Curt holds on.

When class ends, the kids file out without a word. I follow them into the hallway.

"Thanks, kids," I whisper. "See you tomorrow."

"That's cold, Landsman," says Jackie. "That's dog." She's frightened.

When I come back into the room, Jimmy is on the floor, Curt is behind him, still holding him while he kicks out, drums the floor with his feet. I take my next class to the library, and during my prep hour I stay away from the room.

After lunch, Jimmy is still there with Curt's arms around him. They are on the floor and Jimmy has stopped kicking or yelling. Once in awhile he pushes against Curt, and Curt tightens his hold.

Although Jimmy pushes, he doesn't push with all his strength. He rests there against Curt, holding onto Curt's arms, his back against Curt's chest.

I work at my desk. None of us says a word. When I look up, I see that Jimmy has dropped off to sleep. His long lashes fall on his brown cheeks. Curt signals to me to come over. I crouch down across from them.

"Is he awake?" asks Curt.

"He's sleeping," I whisper.

Curt smiles.

He pulls his arms tighter around Jimmy and rests against the wall.

"I'm tired," sighs Curt.

"You can leave him now," I say. "I'll put a jacket under him and he can sleep here."

"Nah. I'll stay with him a while longer."

I hear Curt's quiet voice behind me. "He's always runnin', huh."

"Never stays in one place," I say.

Jackie peeks around the corner and into my room.

"He asleep?" she asks.

"Yep," I say.

"Crazy dude," she says, shaking her head.

"Yep."

She hands me her journal. "You can write back if you want to."

"Thanks," I say.

"Yep," she says, in perfect imitation of my inflection, my tone of voice. "See ya, Landsman."

"See ya, Jackie."

That evening I tell Maury that I am almost at the end of my rope, that I had to get some help today. He offers me the first gin and tonic of the season. I am grateful. The lime smells like perfume.

Aaron comes home quiet and tired after his new afternoon job working at a copy store. He is ready to be done with school himself. We don't say much at dinner. I have begun counting the days until the end of the school year: twenty-five left, including the final teacher work day.

Later, in our bedroom, I read Jackie's journal. There are two short entries.

1. So, there's lots of action at the lakes these nights. Bart helped me move in with Grandma and she didn't get upset, just stared at him the whole time. We sat on her front steps and watched the little kids go by on Big Wheels. But Bart kept standing up, walking out to the sidewalk, coming back. I just wanted to sit but he was ready to go, couldn't sit down. He doesn't touch me much anymore. I don't mind. My grandma seems okay right now. Doesn't like it when I come home late, though. I just can't stay inside. I play bingo at the hall on Blaisdell Avenue. I go to see the fights really. Some of those women really get going. One pulled another by the hair all the way out the door the other day.

2. Jimmy is crazy. He is crazy. He's got to settle down or I might yell at him. He's so cute, too. But he is crazy. He has beautiful skin. I ain't seen too many as bad as him. Even Landsman is getting angry at Jimmy.

My mom would get angry if he was her kid. My grandma says my mom is going to send me a letter soon. I don't know. I'm not sure I want it now. I write Jackie back:

> *Sounds okay at your grandma's. I liked her when I met her. I think she really wants it to work out for you there. If you can just get home by midnight.*
>
> *I hope Jimmy will settle down, too. Sometimes I do feel angry at him, and I guess it is because we're all trying hard, and we'd like it to be an easy spring. We'll see. Thanks for being patient with him.*
>
> *I hope your mom writes soon.*

The day after Jimmy's tantrum, he and I make a plan. If he is ready to settle down and work during most of the class, he can spend ten minutes at the end of the hour with Curt. Jimmy likes this idea. I ask him who he wants to work with on his reading. He smiles and points to Jackie. She willingly moves over next to him.

The class relaxes again. For the next two weeks Jimmy works with Jackie while I help Sandy dictate a short story. I plan lessons for him carefully, some phonics on cards and some puzzles. I give Jackie a book for him to read. He refuses, shaking his head vigorously. She keeps offering him the book each day and finally gets him to look at it, to touch its cover. She puts her arm around the back of his chair, keeping the book out on the table next to them.

Finally one morning, Jackie signals to me.

"Now read it to her," she says. "Go on, read it!"

Jimmy reads two lines from his book. I sit down next to him. We are afraid to look at one another. After two years, wandering in and out of my classroom, he understands the connection between sound and letter, words and meaning. We have struggled with this together, over and over. He has hated me for pushing him. Some mornings I have almost given up. Now he reads, haltingly, but he reads. I love the sound of his voice, struggling over each word. I smile at Jackie, mouthing "thank you" over Jimmy's curly head. She turns away and then signals the rest of the class to be quiet.

Jimmy and I read. The rest of the kids are well behaved, almost solemn. Some of them know how long it has taken Jimmy to get to this place. And they know from the tear that works its way down my cheek that something very important has happened, that Jimmy has begun to find a place in this world.

After class Jackie stands by my desk. Sandy is next to her.

"So. He sounds pretty good, huh, Landsman?"

"He sounds wonderful," I say. "He sounds like he had the best tutor he could have had."

Sandy is quiet. Jackie reaches into her purse and pulls out hers ever-present pack of gum. She offers a stick to Sandy and one to me.

"To celebrate," she says, touching my piece of gum with hers as though they are champagne glasses. She does the same with Sandy's gum.

"Congratulations," I say.

"You too," Jackie responds. She puts her arm around Sandy's waist, and they walk out of my room, laughing.

I invite Curt to come to my classroom at lunchtime to hear Jimmy read. When I come back they are bent over the book together. Jimmy is sounding out each word, each syllable, struggling for meaning. Curt looks on.

After Jimmy has left, Curt says, "He's way behind, ain't he?"

"Yeah. He is. But now he's got the idea. He'll go along fast if he sticks with it."

"I didn't know he was so far behind. Those words are easy words."

"That's where a lot of these kids are."

"You think he'll stop throwin' things now?" asks Curt. He is smiling.

"I sure as hell hope so," I answer.

Curt comes over and puts his arm around my shoulder.

"You too skinny, Landsman."

"These kids work it off me," I say.

"You got more patience than I'd have," says Curt. We are looking out the window.

"I'd just kick 'em out," he says.

"No, you wouldn't," I say.

Curt shakes his head. "Maybe. I don't know." He walks out, repeating, "I just don't know."

I wonder for a moment if I'm too soft, if I should yell at them more. Each spring I question my strength, my toughness. When I first taught, I doubted myself every afternoon. It's after weeks like these, when the weather brings nomads back and the kids are restless, that I wonder how well I'm doing in the classroom.

The next morning I ask the kids to write about a time they experienced a sense of change. Jackie leaves her paper behind for me to read:

> *I changed inside when my mom kicked me out. I changed inside when Derrick put me on the street. I changed inside when Sarah gave me a hug and when you let me work with Jimmy and Mitchell all by myself.*

I change inside when I take drugs, and when my Gram yells at me for being late. I change inside at night, when Bart comes to get me.

I changed once when a man pulled a gun on me.

I don't know what my insides are like any more. I keep changing back and forth.

"I can't believe it," Lesley says. "They say it's the worst kind." She's calling me from a hospital in Indianapolis, sitting on Walter's bed. He is downstairs undergoing additional tests.

"How're you feeling?" I ask.

"Scared," she says.

We are silent, the silence that comes out of confronting death. And we can't even see each other.

"How's Walter?"

"He's pissed. He's just pissed."

"How's Carey?"

"Oh. You know kids. She's confused. Wets her bed every night. New baby coming and this, all at once. It's hard for her to understand any of it. I'll call you when the baby's born," she says and hangs up.

I search through my old photographs. I find one of Lesley, alone, sticking out her tongue, standing in front of our house in Dallas, Texas. We lived there for three years, until my mother could not stand being away from the ocean any longer. Those were the days when we stood on our heads in the bedroom, our undershirts falling away, exposing our bony chests, nipples flat on our skin like golden stars on a chart.

MAY

The last month in school is usually a good time of year for me. I can relax and talk with the kids. But today I keep thinking about Walter.

I snap at Johnny when he won't sit down right away.

"Hey, Landsman, what's goin' on?"

I shrug.

Johnny shrugs in an exaggerated imitation of my body language. He opens his folder, glares up at me, and looks down again.

"So, what's the problem, exactly?" asks Jackie. "You splitting with your husband?"

"Yeah, you splitting? I know a nice man could take you out," says Johnny.

"Naw. She ain't splitting with her husband. 'Member those roses her old man sent her?" says Robert from his corner of the room.

"Oh. Yeah," says Johnny.

"Don't mean nothin'," says Mitchell. "Lotta time they send each other roses right before they split!"

By now, I'm smiling. Sandy looks up from her book.

"So, what's goin' on? We tell you all our stuff."

"Yeah, we do," says Jackie. She pauses. "Well, maybe not *all* our stuff."

Sandy laughs. "That's the truth. Not all of it." They slap hands.

"That's my job," I say, "to listen."

"I listen pretty good," says Johnny.

"My sister is having her second child in a few weeks—" I start.

"And you worried' cause she ain't even married, right?" asks Mitchell.

"Shut up, fool," says Robert.

"Who you callin' fool?" Mitchell stands up.

"You! Fool!" says Robert. They both laugh.

"Shut up you guys. Landsman gets to talk now," yells Jackie.

"So," I say. "Anyway. Lesley, my sister, is married to Walter, and Walter has just found out that he has cancer, and that he's going to die."

"Soon?" asks Johnny.

"Pretty soon," I say.

"Cancer is nasty," begins Johnny. "I know this woman near my house had it. And she was turnin' and moanin' and—"

"Shut up, fool!" says Robert. "Landsman don't need to hear about it."

"So, you goin' to take care of the baby?" asks Sandy.

"As soon as it's born," I say.

"Where your sister live?"

"In Indiana."

"Where's that?" asks Mitchell. "Is it near Vietnam?"

"Naw. Vietnam's near New York," says Johnny. "I know about Indiana. That's where I grew up."

"You didn't grow up in no Indiana," says Robert.

"I did, too. When my mom and daddy were together, I lived there."

"You goin' all the way to Indiana?" asks Jackie.

I get out a map. I show them how close it is.

At this moment Jimmy walks into the room.

"You late, man," says Robert. Jimmy waves a yellow excuse slip and brings it over to my desk. It is signed by his father.

"You living with your dad now?" I ask him.

"Yep. Just moved in last night."

"Man, that's the third time you moved since March," says Jackie. "How you know what direction to go in after school?"

"Some days I get on the wrong bus," Jimmy answers. "Then I run up and down the bus and yell for the driver to let me off." He starts running up and down the room, pretending he is on a bus. I put my head in my hands.

"Shut up, man. Landsman's just now telling us why she's been so bitchy lately."

"Oh yeah?" Jimmy stops in mid-yell. "Why? You splittin' with your old man?"

"Naw," says Mitchell. "She got a sister who's havin' a baby and her sister's old man just got a canker."

"Cancer. Not a canker. He has cancer. You die of cancer," says Robert.

"Oh," says Jimmy. He sits down.

"I used to live in Indiana," says Johnny.

"You didn't live in no Indiana," says Jimmy. "That's all the way out in California!"

"No it ain't, dummy," says Mitchell. He shows Jimmy the map. Jimmy insists on sounding out the word.

"In—di—an—a." It sounds beautiful.

"Oh man," Jimmy slumps in his chair. "I know someone who had cancer. It was dog. His hair fell out."

"Be quiet," yells Sandy. "Just be quiet."

They get back to work, and I listen to Jimmy read until the bell rings. The warmth of his shoulder next to mine is comforting. He struggles so hard these days, dragging out the sounds, putting them together.

After class, Sandy stays behind.

"Rhonda says the Lord takes care of people in pain."

"Thanks. I'll try to remember that."

"You take your time now, and you be all right," she says, and hurries out.

The next day Jackie hands me more journal entries. I take them home and set them aside, then I go out for a run along the river. I can see the water curving, changing, moving in sunlight below me. I'm sure I'm too tired to make the three miles. After the first mile, I warm up and for the rest of the time my body moves well. By the end of the run, I've loosened up, changed gears.

Maury is in the kitchen reading the mail when I come home. His tie is loosened, his jacket on the back of the chair. I kiss him on the top of his head, liking the smell of his hair.

"Long day," he says, pausing for a moment. He leans back against my chest.

I close my eyes and remind myself that his days are tough. I am not the only one who works hard. The sweat is beginning to chill my body. I move, but Maury holds my hands down over his shoulders.

"I'm worried about Lesley."

He nods. "Nothing you can do right now."

"I know." I pull my hands free and head upstairs to shower.

I read Jackie's entries later, after Maury is asleep and Aaron is listening to music downstairs. There are five sections this time:

1. *Hey, Landsman, I'm sorry about your sister and her husband, Love, Jackie.*

2. *My grandma didn't like it when I came in late on Saturday. Bart told me she couldn't do anything to me. But I know she can kick me out. I don't want to be on the streets again. He doesn't seem to think about that, though. It's getting hot outside, too, more fights, people all tense. I don't want to miss it, so I stay out with Bart. But there's knives and booze.*

I wish I could do something right—stay inside and watch television instead of hanging around with Bart. He doesn't hurt me, and he's not asking me to go out and trick for him, but I still don't know if he's good for me. He gets some fine dope, though. When I smoke that stuff I lose track of time and just go along the streets laughing.

3. *Can't last much longer at my grandma's. The old biddy wants me in by midnight. Too much to do out there to come inside early. Bart just wants me to smoke dope with him. I got a job at the old people's home.*

*Some of them are so grouchy and they have that drool on their shirts. But a
lot of them are fun. Like old Mrs. Bennett. She cracks me up, always singing
"You are my sunshine" to me, getting me to smile. And Mr. Camden is
always trying to grab my ass. I've gotten good at slippin out of his way real
fast. He just laughs and says he'll get me next time.*

*4. I'm still here. My grandma said she can't try and keep me in, but
she hasn't kicked me out. And Bart seems happier. Things seem normal. I
have a job and an old man and my grandmother. I've even fixed up my
room a little, bought a spread and a bookshelf. It's nice to have money. The
old people are okay, kind of get on your nerves sometimes, though.*

*This is a story about. I don't got no stories. I liked the one about the
girl and the dress I wrote once.*

*5. I'm out. I just didn't come home Saturday night. Bart and I just
got so stoned we didn't know what we were doing. It's the only way I like
him to touch me, too, when I'm stoned. When I got home that next afternoon my grandmother told me I had to leave. Bart was with me. He just
went outside and sat on the front step, smoked his cigarette. I yelled at my
grandma. I called her all kinds of names. I got my stuff and I left. She just
stood there, smoking and not say in anything. She didn't even care where
I'd stay that night. So, I'm with Bart. He isn't real happy about it and I
don't think I can stay with him too long. I said I'll pay him some rent. He
just laughed. There's another woman down the hall that looks at me funny.
I think I know what's goin on.*

*6. What I really wanted to write about is about the letter my mom
sent last week. She said she was sorry I was gone but maybe it was better.
She never said about Sam or about the day I told her. Now, I know she likes
him better than me. So. That's that, Landsman. That's that. It don't feel
good, thinking about it being that's that. This don't make no sense.*

The house is quiet. The May breeze blows with a sudden coolness
through the windows of the study. I pull my bathrobe around my shoulders. I
don't know what to say to Jackie.

Dear Jackie,

*Hey. I'm sorry about your mom. Damn. I was hoping she would kick
him out and take you back. Maybe we can find another group home for you.
Don't give up. Please. You've been doing so well with us and are such an
important part of the women's group. You are also so good with Jimmy. We
all need you!*

*The job at the old people's home sounds good. I'm sure someone can
give you a reference if you need it.*

*I don't know Bart. But I feel nervous about him; I think that he is
trouble for you. Come talk to me or Jane. We'll try to find you some place
else place else*

Keep writing to me.

Love,
Landsman

I've written a letter, not just a response. I realize that and decide it's okay.
We're about to lose Jackie, and I am frightened for her.

The next morning I make my way into Jane's office after first hour. She
says, before I even bring it up, "I know, Julie. She's on the street again. I just
talked to Mrs. Blakesley."

"She didn't show up in class today. Anything we can do?"

"I'll check on homes. There are a few left."

"Her mother won't take her back. She told Jackie that in a letter."

"Damn. That was another solution." Jane looks weary. May brings runaways in large numbers.

"I'll try to find something," Jane says. "When she comes back, send her
down to me."

It's a beautiful day; the smell of the lilacs, bird song, the smack of the ball
on the field below pour in through the open classroom windows. Frankie quietly sits down next to me at one of the tables. He says nothing, just waits. This
is my prep hour. I don't ask him what class he should be in. I don't say a word.
I like his silent presence, his tattered T-shirt, his new gap-toothed smile. In ten
minutes he gets up and leaves, after running his fingers over the raised gold
stars on his reading chart.

The next day Mom calls to tell me that Lesley had her baby, a boy.
They've decided to name him Loren. I call Lesley's hospital room a day later,
nervous about what to say.

"I'm okay," Lesley says. "You want to talk to Walter? He is sitting here,
holding his son." Her voice is weak.

"Hi, Julie."

"How's the baby doing?" I ask.

"He's big. Big baby. Nine pounds. He looks good," Walter says softly, exhausted himself. "Here's Les."

"You want me to come out?" I ask.

"As soon as you can."

"I'll check plane schedules and call you back."

After I put down the phone, I request a substitute teacher. In a couple of hours I've arranged everything so that I can leave in two days. By then, Lesley will be home.

The next day, I tell the kids that I'll be leaving for a week to take care of my sister.

Johnny puts his thumb in his mouth. Sandy glares at me. Mitchell puts his head down on the desk. Robert stares out the window. Jackie is absent today, the second day in a row.

Surprisingly, Jimmy is the most understanding. "You gotta go, you gotta go, man. That's okay, Landsman."

"Thanks, Jimmy."

Johnny opens his folder. "Don't get us no old white substitute," he says.

"Yeah. Don't get us that old guy we can't understand what he sayin'," says Sandy.

"I'll try to get Bart Campbell," I say.

"Yeah. Get him. He like to talk about sports." Johnny's eyes light up.

At the end of the hour they try extra hard to be sweet as they leave to go to their next class.

"You be nice to that baby, Landsman. You sure you remember how to take care of all that poop and shit?" asks Mitchell.

"Hope your sister ain't too tired," says Sandy. "My sister Lisa wanted to sleep all the time."

"I'll see if I can get her to rest."

"You do that," says Sandy, smiling the wonderful smile that opens up her face. "How her husband?"

"Not good."

"Oh." Sandy stands there looking miserable.

"Could you say good-bye to Jackie for me when she comes back?" I ask her.

"Sure, Landsman. I'll tell her to get her lazy self in here, too."

"Good idea," I say. "Maybe you could call her tonight."

"Yep. I'll call her, if I can find her somewhere."

While I'm mulling over my plans for the substitute teacher, two policemen stop in to ask Ted Marvin about Jackie. They don't say why they are looking for her, only that they need to talk to her. I tell them reluctantly that she hasn't been in school for two days. I finger her last journal entries, read over the letter I wrote to her, which I haven't been able to give to her. I take it, sealed in a manila envelope, to Jane, who says she'll get it to Jackie if she comes back to school. The police have talked to Jane, too. She thinks their presence has something to do with drugs.

Five days later, I arrive home from Lesley's at six o'clock in the evening. There's still enough daylight time left for me to take the run I need, the run that helps me to work through all that I have seen and felt in Indiana.

Walter had emergency surgery just two days after his son's birth while Lesley traveled between the hospital and their small house. Each night Carey wet her bed, and Lesley was too stressed to nurse the baby. There was absolutely no way to lessen the loss for any of them.

One night, while I was in Indiana, Maury called to tell me that Aaron woke him up to talk about smoking dope and trying acid. I listened to this while my new nephew reached his fingers out to the light.

When I was half-asleep on the couch in Lesley's living room, I remember thinking that we know so little, really, about our children or our lovers. I wondered whether I knew more about Jackie and Sandy, Linda and Carol, than I did about Aaron. Had I not welcomed him enough those evenings when he came to say good night? And Maury: had I given up a more intimate life with him, lost to the intensity of being present for the kids I teach?

At my first dinner home, we talk for two hours: about Les and Walter, the babies, LSD, the sixties, catching up on each other's lives.

The next day, I arrive at work an hour before school begins. No one is in our corridor yet, but the kids will be coming through the door soon. I think about how many we've lost.

I remember Nathan, a student I taught two years ago. He had the perfect face to play Huck Finn—blue eyes, freckles, and dark hair. He had been out of school for many days when I decided to find him and talk to him. That day, some of the kids in his class went with me to his house. When Nathan saw us, he ran out the back door and down the back alley, where a pack of dogs prowled the small, wet street near back porches that leaned into the alley. As Nathan ran barefoot in and out of the space between the houses, young men came out into the alley with their dogs to watch.

We finally got him to agree to come back to school late that morning. For months after that he came every day. Once he borrowed a record album from me and returned it unscratched the next day. For a few weeks he read books in class and answered questions. And then one morning he ripped apart my classroom, clawed at the gold stars on his reading chart, kicked at my locked door, screaming obscenities, until one of the men who walks the building carried him down the hall in his arms. The next morning Nathan came back; he looked bewildered by the bits of stars left beside his name. He sat in a corner of the room, his wild hair full of sawdust, his T-shirt full of holes. Over the weeks after that he came less often or came late in the day, barely awake.

Six months later, he attacked a judge during a court session. I've heard that Nathan roams the streets looking occasionally for work.

For a while I believed we could save him. For a while I even believed we could stop Davey from posing in front of movie cameras in downtown warehouses. I tried to keep Jackie safe in school, away from the men who sweet-talk her. But now, after Indiana and the exhaustion of grief, I am disheartened. I realize how little we can do for each other.

When they come in to the classroom, the kids sulk. They show they are glad to see me by refusing to work. They complain about the sub. They tell me that Jackie didn't show up all last week. By the end of the second day, they settle down. In women's group we have a small birthday party for Linda. The highlight of the party is the cake I bought at Target. The icing reads "Happy Birthday" in script. On the top is a small colorful plastic cottage surrounded by colored sugar flowers. We have no paper plates so we use paper towels and kleenex instead. As a surprise for Linda, Jackie appears, looking tired and thin. Her defenses aren't as sharp, her voice not as sure as it was a few weeks earlier.

"I've missed you," I say lightly. I sense that if I push too hard, she'll bolt from the room.

"Yeah, Landsman. I'm comin' back soon."

"Good." I put my hand on her back. She doesn't move away. I can feel her shoulder bone through her black cotton T-shirt.

"You're thin."

"Yeah, well. I ain't eatin' too good."

"You ain't with your grandma no more, huh?" asks Sandy.

"Naw." Jackie shifts uncomfortably, looking at me, looking away.

Then I notice her dirty hands, her smudged and wrinkled slacks.

"There are places we can find for you to sleep," I say. "You can go see Jane again."

She shakes her head, then rests one cheek on her hand, closing herself off with that gesture. The rope of muscle along the side of her neck stands out. She could have been a dancer. She could be anything.

Karen carries Linda's cake into the center of the room. The candles flutter in the breeze from the window. Sandy begins the singing, surprising us all. We join in when Karen sets the cake in front of Linda. Linda smiles, hesitates, then blows all the candles out at once.

"See what you can do if you don't smoke cigarettes," says Jackie, laughing. "I'd take four of those breaths to get those fuckers out!"

I can see Jackie relax into the chair, begin to look around the room.

"That sweet little Jimmy behaving himself?" she asks.

"Oh, yes, he is," says Karen.

"He's okay," I say. "He's doing fine."

"He's so pretty," sighs Jackie.

"I hear his mom's a les," says Linda.

"So," says Jackie.

"So, it's against the Lord's teaching," says Sandy.

"Lotsa things against the Lord's teaching. They get done all the time." Jackie shakes her head. "Lotta devil stuff goes on everywhere."

Sandy shudders slightly and turns away from Jackie.

Someone puts a tape into the player. The sound of Aretha Franklin's voice sets the party mood. Linda cuts the cake, making sure that everyone gets a sugar rose. She carefully sets the small plastic cottage down next to her, then she opens her gifts. The girls compliment her and each other on everything she receives: a T-shirt, costume jewelry, and some chocolate candy.

The party is ordinary. And yet this chips-and-dip party, with music and cake and the kids in their best blouses, is something rare in Linda's life, the only birthday party she has ever had.

When the bell rings, Jackie stays behind. Jimmy sees Jackie from the hall and runs to sit next to her. He rests his head on her shoulder and smiles up at her. She smiles back, resting her hand on his hair for a moment.

"You so pretty, boy!" she says. From anyone else, this would have been reason enough for a fight, a book across the room, chairs knocked over on the floor. From Jackie, it elicits only a playful jab in the shoulder.

"You still readin'?" she asks him.

Jimmy nods his head. He picks up a book lying on the table and opens randomly to a page. He begins to sound out words slowly. Jackie stays near him, concentrating too, putting an arm along the back of his chair as she always did when she worked with him. The final bell rings for group time, and Jimmy jumps up and runs out the door with a quick wave good-bye.

"He sounds pretty good," Jackie says.

"You really helped him."

"Yeah." She smiles weakly. "I did."

"Jane can talk to you about finding another home. Let's go down."

"Naw. I'm doin' fine."

"Come see her and just say hello," I say. "I left some things with Jane I wrote to you the last time you were in class."

Jackie shrugs her shoulders but comes with me. In Jane's office Jackie reaches eagerly into the candy jar and grabs a caramel. She sits across from Jane, leaning back, eyes closed, the caramel in her mouth.

"Will you give her the envelope before she goes?"

"Sure."

"So," I can hear Jane saying as I leave, "we need to find you somewhere else, huh?"

I stop off at Ted Marvin's office to tell him about Jackie. He listens, nods his head, asks about Lesley, and we talk for a few minutes about her kids, about cancer, about Indiana. I'm happy to sink down in the chair across from him, to take the time to fill him in on the last week.

Later, standing at my classroom window, I see Jackie walking past the athletic field. She notices me and waves. She stops in front of a young man who bends to light her cigarette. He says something to her, then walks away toward Lake Street, where there are lots of places to hang out. She turns to see if I am still there, her cigarette resting between her fingers, hand on her hip.

She waves again, then turns and walks away, heading in the same direction for Lake Street. I call Jane on the school phone to find out what happened at their meeting. She has calls in to group homes.

"I tried to convince Jackie to go to the emergency shelter for tonight, but she bolted. Keep in touch," she tells me. "It's so damn hard to find anything for them, this time of year."

I sit back at my desk. Right now I don't have much hope for Jackie or much belief that this system can respond to the needs of kids who are running from pimps or are afraid of their fathers. The kids disappear because we don't have enough of the right places for them to stay when they are under attack. They need safety and stability at least as much as they need algebra.

Rhonda calls me at home to say that she has a present for me. After school on Friday, I drive over to her apartment and find Sandy waiting on the front step. The day is flat and hot, a spring day when the heat shimmers along Blaisdell Avenue. Small children crouch over tricycles, pushing them through the uncut grass. A man leans against his car, smoking, talking to his buddy on the sidewalk. I cannot imagine his willingness to add the heat of that burning cigarette to the heat that surrounds him from the buildings.

Sandy stands up to greet me. Unlike the other young women in shorts who saunter by, arguing singsong about their boyfriends, she wears a skirt. Yet her posture is not as stiff as usual. Her body seems loose, almost relaxed. On the phone, Rhonda mentioned that Sandy has refused to go to church in the evenings.

"Hi," she says, suddenly shy, unsure of herself.

"Hi," I respond. "What's this present? I can't imagine!" I say, chattering nervously, catching Sandy's discomfort.

"You'll see, Landsman," says Sandy, smiling now.

We walk up the steps together, across a wide porch and upstairs to the second floor where Rhonda is waiting. The living room is darkened and closed in by velvet chairs, rose red walls, lots of woodwork, and heavy green drapes. There are icons everywhere and pictures of the kids, Sandy and Lisa at every stage of their growing up. Jasmine is holding onto a glass-topped coffee table, tottering as though she is on a rolling ship, unable to keep her legs firmly on the floor. She looks up at me, her brown skin shiny, her eyes large under tiny, perfectly beaded braids.

Rhonda gives me a hug, the first time she's ever done that, and I almost dissolve in her strong arms. I let her hold me for a moment. Sandy shifts behind us, uncomfortable with this blurring of categories in her life.

"Show her the present," she says.

Rhonda leads me into the kitchen.

"I don't know why I suddenly remembered this," Rhonda says, smiling. "But I woke up the other morning and thought about the time Sandy told me your favorite dessert was pineapple upside-down cake." I remember the talk we had during a women's group meeting about our favorite foods. Rhonda reaches into the refrigerator and brings out the round cake, exactly like the ones my mother made for me every birthday: whole pineapple rings embedded in a crust of hardened brown sugar, a glazed cherry in the middle of each ring.

I am overcome. All I can do is smile and nod my head. I turn to Rhonda and hug her again, gathering myself together right there in her arms.

Over her shoulder I see Sandy. She is smiling the smile that softens her face, that beautiful opening up of her eyes.

"Now you take this home to your family," says Rhonda, putting the cake into a round plastic carrying case.

"And here's the whipped cream to go along with it." She hands me a small silver bowl.

"I'm really surprised," I manage to blurt out. "This is so unexpected."

"It's the Lord's way of talking to me, telling me what to do."

Sandy invites me into the living room with her. We sink into the deep velour couch. She reads aloud to me, perfectly, with speed and fluency, from the New Testament. Our shoulders are touching, the first time she has let me come so close. Rhonda sits across from us, holding Jasmine on her lap. The room is stifling. Sweat runs down my arms, my skirt clings to the back of my legs. Sandy reads on for ten minutes before she closes the heavy Bible. I have become drowsy, so that the familiar words from boarding-school days have the rhythm of a song.

"You sound wonderful," I say, leaning back into the couch, not wanting to leave.

Sandy nods her head, obviously proud.

"What a difference from this fall." I smile at her.

"She reads just fine, now. Thank you, and thank the Lord for teaching her," says Rhonda.

I don't argue about the Lord's part in this. I don't need more credit than Rhonda has given me. Whatever the forces are that have brought Sandy to this point are just fine with me.

"Sandy's worked real hard in class," I say. And she has. I wonder if she's been practicing her reading on those evenings she's been staying home from church.

"It's her time," says Rhonda, rocking Jasmine in her lap. Jasmine's eyes are closed. Her cheek rests on Rhonda's shoulder. Outside, cicadas shriek, loud and insistent.

Remember this moment, I think, no matter what, remember Rhonda's skin, Jasmine's cheek, Sandy's happiness. Let yourself take some small amount of credit for this, some small amount of hope from it.

"How's your sister?" asks Rhonda, as though she can see my exhaustion, my unwillingness to leave.

"Oh. Thank you for asking. Her husband is really sick." I get up, sensing what's coming. I don't want to hear Rhonda talk about the Lord.

"The Lord works in some stange ways," she says, nodding her head for emphasis. She rocks Jasmine, humming a song under her breath.

Sandy returns from the kitchen with the cake and the bowl of whipped cream.

"I'll walk you down," she says.

"Thank you so much," I say. "This will be a perfect way to start the weekend." My blouse clings to my back.

"You take care of yourself," says Rhonda. She holds out her right hand, the baby draped over her left shoulder.

I shake her firm hand. "You too. I'll give the cake pan back to Sandy in school."

"Don't worry about it," she says, sitting back down and rocking Jasmine again.

"You take care," I say to Sandy, who, out in the afternoon heat, has straightened to her full height.

In the rearview mirror I can see her walking slowly back to the porch. I carefully anchor the cake on the front seat with my bag. I hear Bible verses in my head. I want to sing them, softly, add music to the gift, add dance.

During most of the next week, Jackie does not show up at school. The kids say they've seen her in the park. Johnny says she's been beaten up. Finally, on Friday, she appears the last hour of the day for women's group. The skin around her eye is swollen and yellowing. Her arms are scratched where she digs into them with her fingernails. Her hair is dirty, and her skin has a gray, unhealthy look. Her voice is hoarse.

"You look bad, girl," says Carol. In typical nomad fashion, Carol has come back after weeks on the reservation and wants to begin school where she left off.

"So? You do what you gotta do," says Jackie. She shrugs.

"You don't gotta get beat up," says Sandy. "Nobody's gotta do that!"

"Sometimes that's the way it goes," says Jackie. She has not looked at me since she walked in.

"You need to get away from that ol' pimp of yours," says Carol.

"He ain't no pimp. He's my man," says Jackie. She turns her chair so that she is facing away from the group and can look out the window.

They do not try to argue with her. Instead they ignore Jackie, let her sit with them and listen to their discussion. They are having trouble with teachers now, are bad-mouthing them, are often asked to leave their classes. I want them to practice different ways of approaching their teachers, so we role-play some situations. One of them takes the part of the teacher, another, the student.

They amaze me with the accuracy with which they portray my colleagues, right down to the tone of voice, mannerisms, accents. They laugh at each other, yet take the exercise seriously, rehearsing for the next week. Graduation is close, and some of them have a chance to pass all their classes this trimester.

After three role-plays, Carol invites Jackie to join them.

"I don't got no teachers now," says Jackie.

"Yeah, but you can act like one so we can practice," says Linda.

"I'll do Landsman," Jackie says, slowly getting out of her chair.

"We get along with Landsman," says Sandy. "You don't need to do her."

"That's okay, I'd like to see myself," I say. Jackie smiles at me for the first time all day. She walks over and stands at the door.

"Somebody be the bell ringing," she says.

"R-r-r-ing!" yells Carol. "R-r-r-ing!"

Jackie starts toward the desk. Then she stops, looks around, turns toward a bookshelf, begins to straighten some books, stops suddenly, looks toward the door, runs over to it, stops, turns back toward the desk, runs over to it, lifts up papers, looks under them, looks up, looks back down at the desk, opens my grade book, flips through it, runs back over to the door, comes back to the desk.

By now all of us are laughing. Jackie has demonstrated exactly what I do when the bell rings. In the five minutes between classes I must look crazed, trying to say good-bye to the past hour kids, pick up the room a little, prepare folders for the next class to begin, stand in the hall to monitor traffic and welcome the next hour kids. Jackie has my frantic pace, my perplexed look down perfectly. She collapses into my chair, laughing with us.

"Okay, Landsman, you do Jackie now," says Sandy.

"No, that's okay. I couldn't follow that act," I say somewhat nervously.

"Then be her pimp," says Carol. "Jackie got no teachers, but she got a pimp she tryin' to get rid of." She turns to Jackie. Jackie shrugs her shoulders, takes out a stick of gum and offers the pack around.

"I don't care. Go ahead," she says, looking at me.

"Okay," I say. I take a deep breath. The kids are quiet.

"You start, Landsman. You tell me to get out on the streets."

"Okay." I wait a minute. The kids giggle and then stop.

"Come on, baby," I say. "Come with me. You know I can take care of you. You know that, baby. I got a nice room, clothes, plenty of cigarettes, good dope."

I have the inflection down when I talk to her. I am not sure why or how I've absorbed it, but I surprise myself with the way I sound.

"I ain't comin' with you no more," says Jackie. She sounds wooden, unconvincing, separated from the role of herself.

"Yes, you are, girl. You know you need me, baby. You can't make it out here without me."

"I got me a job at the old people's home," Jackie says, a little fight in her voice.

"Shit, girl! That don't mean nothin'. That pays shit, girl. You still be out in the cold without your daddy here."

The kids have stopped smiling. They are listening intently.

"Don't matter what it pays, man. And hey! I don't get this from the old people," says Jackie, pointing to her swollen eye.

"Oh, baby, that was just a one-time thing," I say. "I got my temper up. It's what happens some time."

"It won't happen to me," says Jackie. "I ain't goin' out on those streets again."

"Yeah, you is, Jackie. You got to." I make my voice angry, threatening.

"I don't got to," she says, sitting up straight, glaring at me. "I don't got to do nothin' for you." She chews her gum loudly. She doesn't move a muscle. No one in the room seems to be breathing.

I glare back at Jackie. "You think so, baby. You think you can keep yourself in cigarettes, but you can't. You come on now and you'll have a vacation for a few days and stay warm and get high."

My voice is commanding her.

"Forget that shit," says Jackie. "Vacation, shit! You just keep me locked up. You talk about your ol' vacations."

"Hey, girl. Don't make me angry," I say, my voice hard. "You know how I am when you make me angry."

"Don't you threaten me none," she says. "I ain't goin' out for you." She keeps her voice steady. I can feel her fear now. The kids are watching us, their eyes moving from one of us to the other.

"I'm comin' back," I say. "I ain't leavin' you for long. And when I come back, you better be ready."

"I ain't never goin' to be ready for you!" says Jackie.

I get up and walk toward the door. I turn as I get to it. I shake my fist at her.

"Shit, girl, you don't know nothin'! You won't be able to make it without your daddy here. You jus' be ready when I come back."

"I never be ready for you," says Jackie, voice cocky, almost arrogant. Her cheeks are flushed, eyes bright.

When I walk out the door, the class erupts in cheers. The girls are congratulating Jackie, slapping her palms. I sit with them, exhausted. I am frightened by the intensity in the room, by the power of the group, of my own role. Jackie smiles at me and leans back in her chair.

"You showed him, girl," says Carol.

"You sure did," says Sandy.

"Hey, Landsman. How you know so much about pimps?" asks Carol. "You must've known some pimps in your time." The girls laugh.

"She knew Anthony," says Jackie. "He's got all the moves."

"That's true, he does," I say, pleased that Jackie has figured out the source of my knowledge.

"You think you'll really do that?" asks Sandy.

"Do what?" asks Jackie.

"Do what you just did with Landsman."

Jackie shrugs. "I don't know. My man ain't really my pimp."

"Oh, girl," says Carol. "It don't matter if you don't call him that. Jus' get rid of the man!"

The girls laugh. Jackie does, too.

Then Linda asks to do a role-play. She has been so quiet that I am surprised to hear her speak.

"You just guess who this is," she says. She gets up, walks to the wall near the door of my room, stands up against it and folds her arms across her chest. She stares at us all.

The girls call out, "Mr. Marvin!" immediately and in unison.

"Yep." It was a perfect pose, exactly the way Ted stands, feet somewhat apart, a businesslike look on his face.

Carol does a perfect imitation of Curt, lumbering down the hall heading straight for some kid who is running away frantically.

When the bell rings, the rest of the girls run out of the room, ready for the weekend, but Jackie waits. She knows I want her to see Jane about a place to stay, and she seems willing.

Jane is still at her desk working, her curly brown hair barely visible behind the stacks of folders on her desk. She smiles at Jackie and offers her a chair.

"How about St. Joseph's Shelter?" she asks Jackie.

"Okay. I'll try it, I guess."

I turn to leave the crowded room and Jackie says, "Thanks, Landsman, you make some fine pimp!"

"Any time," I answer and close the door softly.

That evening I arrive home after dinner with a friend, an hour and a half spent laughing, talking about kids and husbands. Maury meets me at the kitchen door. I can hear the television on upstairs.

"It's Walter?" I ask, knowing the answer.

I take the next day off from school. I know I'll need the kids tomorrow, but today I cry. I cry for all the places that Walter never got to see, for the motorcycle races and the canoe trips he loved. I cry for my sister, for her loneliness, for a baby waiting for her attention, oblivious to the events around him, and for Carey, who had so few years with her father.

I think about Jackie choosing to hide out rather than go back to the step-brother who waited outside the door to her bedroom, finding places to sleep when the winter came. I remember her description of the fight on Franklin Avenue, her pimp going down. I remember the knife that caught the light in a room in D. C., and the one in my classroom a few months ago. I think about Lesley and Walter, about the courage it takes to make it in this world.

I make reservations to fly out for the funeral.

In school on Tuesday I don't tell the kids about Walter's death. I want the day to move along like any other. A new student, Bill, is sent to my room. He is withdrawn, speaks to no one, and has hurt his mother seriously a couple of times. While I am busy with him, the others get restless as they always do when a new student shows up. Suddenly, they can't seem to work on their own. A day before they were reading quietly to themselves, working on vocabulary or writing. Now they raise their hands constantly and whine like toddlers.

And this, I realize, after the hour is finally over, this is exactly what I need. I am exhausted, but I feel that I've had a good workout, that I have earned my pay.

The same day I leave for the funeral, I stop in to set up work for the substitute teacher who will take my classes. When the first hour students arrive, I tell the kids why I am leaving.

"When you be back, Landsman?" asks Mitchell.

"On Tuesday."

"Okay."

The rest of the kids slump in their chairs. They are angry. It doesn't matter why I am leaving them, I am leaving them. And at the same time they know how I feel and they try to respond.

"You got to go to the funeral?"

"I'll get there just in time."

"I don't like funerals," says Mitchell. "All that bawlin'."

"But at least our funerals be better than white funerals!" says Johnny.

"Be quiet now," says Sandy, looking at me.

"I'm sorry, Landsman." He puts his head down on the table.

"What's wrong with white funerals?" asks Linda, who has come in to say good-bye.

"They so quiet," says Sandy.

"They're civilized," says Linda.

"You sayin' we ain't civilized?" asks Johnny.

"Quiet," says Sandy. "Landsman don't need no fightin' today."

"See you Friday," I say.

"See you Friday," Johnny answers back.

It is hard to leave them.

When I come back this second time from Indiana, Maury and Aaron meet my plane and take me to dinner. Aaron is more animated than I have seen him in a while. He has only a week left of tenth grade. These last few months he has been struggling to get through school, hating the windowless building, the pep fests, classes taught by teachers who are counting the few years until retirement. His favorite class is ceramics, where he retreats the third period of each day to throw pots.

"I think I've got the hang of the wheel," he says. "Winslow just leaves us alone. It's great, like meditation."

"Can you bring home some of what you make?" I ask.

"Sure, next week, right before we get out. Shit, man! Next week! I'm done *next week!*" He looks as though he wants to get up and dance on the table.

Maury smiles at me, at Aaron. He's had to take on a lot more of the housework this past month, and his own job has been demanding.

"Come on, guys, get excited!" says Aaron. "Mom, you're almost done, too!"

"Yeah, that's true," I say. "I've barely noticed."

"Well, notice, man! The summer. I mean the whole fuckin' summer!" He yells. He throws one arm up in the air.

"Aaron. Everyone's looking at us!" I say, laughing, beginning to feel what he's feeling. The wine, my relief at being home, and Maury and Aaron's excitement fill my body.

"Any calls from school?" I ask as we walk toward the car.

"Just Rhonda. She wants to know what time the graduation ceremony is."

"Oh, Yeah," I say remembering that we have to plan the food and the certificates. I realize how much I am looking forward to seeing the kids, to finding out how Johnny has done with the new book I left for him, whether Sandy behaved herself, and if Jackie stopped back to visit and is still at the shelter. After the intensity of these last days, I'll enjoy working on details: finding a speaker for the ceremony and buying paper cups for punch.

I head for the bedroom to unpack and to try, for a while, to keep the confusion and sadness of the last few days out of my mind so that I can fall asleep.

Maury comes upstairs. He sits on the edge of the bed watching me take out clothes and hang what I didn't use.

"Aaron seems wonderful," I say.

"He's fine," Maury says. "I'm fine."

Something is left unsaid.

"What's wrong?" I say. "Are you angry?"

"No. Not angry. I just want you to know we survive without you. We don't enjoy it, but we make it."

"What else?" I ask, sitting next to him.

"Nothing. Except. Your school kids will survive, too, Jules."

I feel an inexplicable relief at his words. They find a place in me that feels new.

"Thanks, sweetheart," I say.

"Not that we like it when you're gone. Even the dog whines a lot. I whine a lot. Aaron didn't whine so much. He's really flying."

I get out of my clothes and into my nightgown. It's only nine-thirty, but I'm ready for bed. Maury wanders to the study to watch the news. I drift off, trying not to think about Lesley.

JUNE

*"All our children ought to be allowed a stake
in the enormous richness of America. Whether
they were born to poor black people in the Bronx
or to rich people in Manhasset or Winnetka, they
are all quite wonderful and innocent when
they are small. We soil them needlessly."*

—Jonathan Kozol, *Savage Inequalities*

When I return to school the kids in first hour are excited, unwilling to sit down, barely noticing that I'm back after four days. Curt takes Jimmy out for doughnuts. Johnny asks if he can be excused to help the gym teacher set up for a field day. Robert stands at the window, unable to sit. Jackie isn't there.

"So, how did it go while I was away?" I ask Sandy and Mitchell, who are at their usual places, their folders open.

"Oh, fine, Landsman. We had that ol' white sub, but we did fine anyways," says Mitchell, barely looking at me.

"Yeah. Only Jimmy tried some stuff at first, but Curt took care of him."

"Well, good," I say.

"How was the funeral?" asks Mitchell.

"Sad," I say. "It's hard when there are little kids left without their dad."

"How old are the kids?" asks Sandy.

"Carey's four, Loren's a month."

"Ooooooh, that's real sad," says Sandy, shaking her head.

Johnny runs into the room, his shirt hanging out of his belt and his pants grass-stained. I've never seen Johnny messed up, his every seam not straight. A boy about twice his size follows him.

"I'm sorry, man," says Johnny, holding up his arms to keep the boy from getting ahold of him. Johnny is laughing. "I'm sorry, Patrice, man, I didn't mean it."

Patrice is smiling too. He comes right over to Johnny and puts both hands on his head, pushing him down in the chair, but gently, so Johnny won't be hurt.

"You sayin' some cold things about my woman, man."

Johnny looks up at Patrice. "Okay, okay. I was just talkin'." Then he giggles.

Patrice turns away and walks out of the room.

"I thought you were supposed to be helping out there," I say.

"Aw, Landsman, I didn't mean nothin' about his girl-friend." Johnny puts his thumb in his mouth.

This is the fragmented time, the very end of the year. The kids are excited, yet nervous about leaving for the summer. I always struggle during these days. I look for movies or field trips, something to get us through. Today, I get out Claude Brown's *Manchild in the Promised Land* and read aloud to them. An unusually warm June morning settles around us. Robert turns toward the group, listening. Johnny sucks his thumb. Mitchell rests his head on one arm, while Sandy leans back in her chair. When Jimmy comes in carrying a white paper bag from Dunkin' Donuts, he salutes and sits down without saying a word.

As I read, I begin to relax with them. I feel relieved at the familiar way this works, the storytelling, the words spoken out loud.

When the bell rings, no one moves. I keep reading for another minute to finish the paragraph.

" 'See you tomorrow,' I say. "I'll finish the chapter then."

After they've left, I realize that I miss Jackie. She would have listened while pushing her hair back behind one ear. She might have doodled on her notebook.

We all miss her. The kids say she's planning to come to the graduation ceremony to visit and to see her friends.

The next day Jackie appears for first hour. She says she's found her own place and still has her job with the old people. I'm not sure I believe her but I don't question her. Her face has healed, and her hair is clean. She says she misses us all. Her hands pull at the chain on her pink plastic purse. One small muscle below her eye twitches. She glances nervously out the door, out the window.

"What's the matter with you, girl? You afraid someone comin'?" asks Sandy, watching Jackie intently.

"Her man mad at her for leavin' his crib," says Johnny.

"Shut up, boy," Jackie says.

"Leave her alone," says Robert quietly from the back of the room. He has been putting in time in school, waiting to get out, to get on with his life. He's had a pretty good year with us.

Jackie gives him a grateful smile. "I need to find me a better job," she says. "Or another job for the nights. The old people home don't pay nothin'."

"Who at your crib? You share it?" asks Mitchell.

"Some friend of Carol's needed a place to crash. Can't pay me no rent yet, though. She don't got no job, either."

"They need people at that new pizza place on Lake Street," says Sandy.

"Maybe I'll go over there. I don't like pizza so much, though," says Jackie, wrinkling up her nose.

"You crazy, girl! You don't like pizza!" Sandy is shocked.

"She like steak, right, Jackie? You like a big ol' steak with baked potato and sour cream?" Johnny asks, almost drooling.

"You right about that, little boy," says Jackie, putting her hands around his face and giving him a kiss on the forehead. He chuckles, then quickly, before she can stop him, he kisses her on the cheek. She leans back and looks at him for a long moment.

"Boy, you so cute someone gonna snatch you up and carry you home."

The entire class laughs. Johnny puts his thumb in his mouth.

When everyone else leaves, Sandy and Jackie stay behind.

"You lookin' better," says Sandy.

"I'm scared, though."

"You got a lock?"

"Ain't got no phone. That really makes me scared."

"Maybe your grandmother could give you some money—just for the phone," I suggest.

Jackie looks thoughtful for a moment.

"She just might." Her face brightens a little. Jackie seems so lost, so down, that the simplest possible solutions escape her.

Ted Marvin stops by. He asks Sandy to help him with some envelopes he needs addressed.

"That mean I can miss home ec class?"

"I've cleared it with your teacher."

"Fine," says Sandy. "I'll come along in a minute."

"Good to see you here," he says to Jackie before he leaves. There is no need for him to play the tough administrator now.

Jackie gets up. "I gotta go. Maybe I'll stop by and see my grandma."

"You comin' to graduation?" asks Sandy as they head toward the hallway.

"Don't know. Maybe." They leave together, Sandy, tall and broad, heading for Marvin's office, Jackie still too thin, her body with its slight curves heading down the stairs.

The last week goes quickly with final tests and the end of the year celebration on the last day. We always hold a ceremony for those who are going on to new schools or to the next grade level, and at that time we award certificates to students for achievement and progress. All the students in the program are invited. We invite a formal speaker, too, often from the school board. The weather is usually hot and humid, so we keep the actual celebration quite brief.

Our students have invited uncles and aunts, mothers and fathers, sisters and brothers, and guardians. Johnny hopes that his mother will show up. Robert says he doesn't think anyone is coming from his family. Sandy proudly tells us that Rhonda will be there, and Jasmine, too. Maybe even her sister, Lisa. I've given Mitchell an invitation to bring to his mother, but he keeps his head down during this talk, Jimmy says that his dad may come, but he doesn't know. Linda has invited her grandmother.

The last day of school is sweltering. The prairie heat that settles on this flat city barely lifted last night. As I drive to work I can feel yesterday's heaviness steaming from each building. On Franklin Avenue, men are lined up on the sidewalk outside of Dick's Bar, waiting for it to open. An old car, stripped of its tires, rests at an angle in the alley near school.

In the hallways, I feel the excitement of the last day. I prepare myself to confiscate squirt guns, interrupt arguments, calm fears. I feel like a student myself, getting ready to go away for the summer.

When I open the door to my room at 7:15 A.M., the students are already there. They must have asked the custodian to let them in early. Amazingly, Jackie is here, wearing high heels and a pink pantsuit that looks as if it has been sprayed onto her body. Her face is pale, but she has no new bruises. Johnny sports a flower in the lapel of his three-piece pin-striped suit. Sandy's long black dress is finished off with a round white collar. A red rose is pinned on the collar right near her throat. Robert looks much more formal than usual in a white sports jacket, blue shirt, and maroon tie. Even Mitchell has managed a new shirt and gray slacks. Linda is unexpectedly present, too, in a turquoise shirt and white jeans. The kids have arranged doughnuts and cans of pop on two tables they have pushed together in the front of the room.

"You look bad, Landsman," says Johnny approvingly. I am wearing a black knit top with a flowered skirt, stockings, and very uncomfortable open-toed high heels.

"Thanks, Johnny." I sit down at the table with them.

We talk: desultory, easy conversation about the summer, their plans, next fall. Jimmy, as usual these days, comes in late, Curt right behind him.

"Sorry he's late," says Curt. "We had to do a little shopping."

Jimmy smiles. He has on new jeans and a clean shirt. He points to his feet. He is wearing new Nike running shoes.

"Ah hah!" I say. "And how is anyone going to be able to catch him now?"

"Yeah. Well. That's a problem," says Curt.

Jimmy sits down and gulps a Coke.

The room is more peaceful than it's ever been, even on the best of days.

"I'm goin' to Indiana in July, to see my daddy. Don't like his wife, though," says Johnny.

"I don't like my mama's new boyfriend either," says Mitchell.

"Men can be lots of trouble," says Jackie.

I am content not to lead this discussion. I am pleased to sit here and look at the kids. I often forget how handsome they are. I am usually too concerned with their reading, the amount of work they've done, or how long they've been able to sit in their seats. I am always keeping track of their points or their worksheets or extra credit assignments. Now they sit in front of me in their best clothes. Mixed with the excitement of getting out of school is their fear of what the summer at home will be like, how they will cope with the streets, their relatives, new men in their homes.

"Who you goin' to live with this summer?" Robert asks Jimmy.

"My mom, I think," he answers.

"I'm goin' to try and live with my grandmother," says Linda. "I don't know. We never got along so good before."

"I'm stayin' right here, in my own place," says Jackie, cracking her gum.

"You got another job?" asks Sandy.

"Not yet. I filled out applications, though, and I added a few more hours at the home."

"I'm goin' to Indiana," says Johnny.

"We know that. You already said that. You just sayin' it again' cause Landsman was there."

"No. I ain't. I really do go there!"

Johnny makes a move with the lower part of his body as though he is going to get up out of his chair. But he doesn't even rise to his feet.

No one challenges him. No one challenges anyone. They are dressed too nicely.

I read aloud to them from the end of *Manchild* for the last fifteen minutes. The bell rings. First hour is over for the year.

The ceremony takes place in a classroom next to mine. During lunch the staff sets up the room. We carry in a long table, a podium, and extra chairs. For the next hour, the students walk around visiting teachers, saying good-byes, catching a last cigarette outside the door.

At exactly 1:30 P.M., dressed in a navy suit and white sleeveless blouse, Rhonda comes and sits down in the back row. She has come alone, without Lisa or Jasmine. She fans herself with a piece of paper. Mitchell's mother, Audrey Davis, arrives and takes a seat by the window. I remember the stories the kids told about her ambush of Mitchell at the roller-skating rink. Now she sits, smiling at Mitchell as he walks over. Audrey reaches up and buttons the top button of his shirt. Everyone is dressed up except one man who staggers as he walks, slumps into a chair, and falls back, snoring loudly. His shirt is tattered, and his pants are covered with dirt. He is the father of a student who has already left for North Dakota. He does not even know that she has gone. Several people try unsuccessfully to wake him up to explain this to him.

While the parents arrive, many of them ill at ease in a school building, the scene of so many difficult moments for their kids, Linda stands at the stairs, waiting. She needs her grandmother today, some sign that asking her to spend the summer is not simply an obligation.

Johnny's mother walks in looking like a model—dressed in high heels, a tight denim skirt, and a white silk blouse. Her hair is braided. She sits down quickly in an aisle seat. Johnny walks up to her cautiously, and, smiling at him, she picks a thread off the collar of his suit jacket.

I keep looking for Jimmy's father or mother. He has made such progress this year. He is looking, too, but tries to hide the fact that he is waiting for anyone. He keeps glancing at the door, then away. Curt pokes at him playfully, then looks at me. Both of us have had our fingers crossed that someone would show up for Jimmy. No one does.

To Robert's surprise, his mother appears with his three-year-old daughter, Katisha. He sits next to them, his daughter on his lap. Katisha is dressed up in yellow ruffles. It is good to see the seriousness with which everyone takes this ceremony, the effort they put into dressing and coming to school in this unbearable heat.

Jackie slides in next to Robert and Katisha. She is really here as a friend, as a relative. She offers Katisha a piece of gum. The little girl takes the gum from Jackie, staring at her the whole time. Jimmy has slumped down in his seat, realizing that neither of his parents is going to come. Jackie changes seats, moves next to him, puts her arm around him. He rests his head on her shoulder and closes his eyes.

I look around. I miss the nomads: Carol and her honesty, Karen and Davey, Anthony in his pimp clothes.

Finally, Ted Marvin begins the program with a brief welcome. I stand at the back of the room, increasingly uncomfortable in the heat. A school board member, Mr. Watkins, makes a speech. He knows our program well, so his speech about self-discipline is short. The kids manage to sit quietly until he finishes and congratulates them.

This has been a long year. When I think about the behavior of most of the kids when they first came in and compare it with what I see now, I am impressed. I don't know what will stick, of course, what they can maintain. Sandy is really on her way. One more year in the program and her face will lose those anger lines. She has Rhonda and God and a fierce sensitivity. She has Jasmine and her sister and a strong sense of what is right. I wonder, though, about her need to be touched, about how that hungry part of her will be satisfied.

And Johnny. Johnny will jump over fences to get away from cops once in a while this summer. And he may run up against the wrong person some hot afternoon on Plymouth Avenue when the men are shooting dice. Curt says that Johnny writes too many checks with his mouth, and that someday someone is going to cash them for him. That may be true. But he reads better than he did in the fall, and I do believe he's grown a little this spring. Maybe spending July in Indiana will keep him safe part of the time.

Jackie, in her gold hoop earrings and her glass heels, hugs Jimmy. Pink brings out the flush in her cheeks, the freckles that brush her nose. In a last journal entry she handed me this morning, she wrote me a note of goodbye:

> *"Landsman, Here's my new address—2203 Stevens Avenue. No phone but you can stop by. I don't know if I'll be able to keep the place unless I find more money. Someone saw Bart in my neighborhood.*
>
> *My grandma gave me a check for my phone deposit. Thanks for the idea. She says I can visit her when I want. My mom wants to see me. I don't know.*
>
> *I'm still sorry about your sister's husband.*
>
> *Maybe I'll write you this summer. Maybe I'll come back in the fall. I have some more parts to the story about the girl and the dress.*
>
> *You be good. I'll look for you out at Lake Nokomis. Or downtown.*
>
> > *Love,*
> >
> > *Jackie.*

She turns in her seat, restless. Jimmy moves away from her. I watch her face close up to a hardness she must use on the street.

Linda will try living with her grandmother again. She has a job in the suburbs, filing and addressing envelopes for a travel agency. Her father is locked up for the time being, so she has some breathing space.

Jimmy may have a hard time remembering where he lives, may continue to strut up and down the aisle of the bus, asking the driver to let him off. The kids say he was picked up for shoplifting the other night; he stole a shirt and some designer jeans. He's still got that anger, that strut, the need to dance on table tops. Yet he has learned to read. He was even able to pick out a birthday card for his mother for the first time, a card whose message he could read and understand. I just don't know about Jimmy.

Mitchell will hang out at the projects, watch men shoot dice, and run away if knives start catching sunlight in front of his eyes. He'll probably stay out all night, and his mother will probably find him the next morning, bring him home, keep him in the apartment for days. Audrey will keep him safe most of the summer. The kids say he's going to dance in a contest. If he wins, he'll earn some money and a chance to be on television.

Robert has earned most of his high school credits. He'll go to summer school and graduate next fall. If he can keep his temper, he'll go into the Marines and do well there. I'll miss him because he was as close to an adult as anyone I've ever taught, and he knew how to be helpful in that adult way.

Curt stands up and acts as the emcee. He obviously enjoys awarding the prizes.

"For perfect attendance: Johnny Washington." Johnny walks up to the front, looking serious. I guiltily remember the many times I wished he'd be absent just once! Yet he couldn't have made the progress he's made without coming every day. Maybe next year he'll be ready to take his thumb out of his mouth. As soon as Johnny sits down, Curt calls his name again. "Johnny Washington, for accomplishment in reading!" Johnny sees me standing in the back of the room and bows toward me. His mother laughs outright along with the others who whistle and cheer as he gets his second certificate. Curt shakes Johnny's hand, and Mr. Watkins does, too. Johnny does a little dance step as he walks back down the aisle. His mother puts her arm around him when he settles in again.

"For most improvement in reading, Jimmy Shadow." The kids clap loudly as Jimmy ducks his head and walks up front to accept his award. He doesn't smile. In his T-shirt and jeans he looks quite thin, quite exposed. Curt hands Jimmy his certificate and holds on to his hand a long time when they connect. He looks huge next to Jimmy. Curt deserves a piece of this award, as does Jackie.

"Now," says Curt, "a certificate for best tutor goes to Jackie Simmons."

Jackie stays in her seat, shaking her head. She looks back at me, and I am startled by what seems like fear in her eyes. The kids are pushing her to accept the award. Jimmy pulls at her hand, urging her forward. Mitchell whispers something to her, and his mother puts her hand on Jackie's shoulder. After what seems like minutes, she gets up and walks to the front of the room on those high glass heels. The boys whistle loudly and stamp their feet. Jackie is blushing, shaking her head, her hair falling over one eye. Mr. Watkins stands up to congratulate her. He takes her ringed fingers in his and firmly shakes her hand. When she turns around she is smiling, and there is nothing tough about that smile.

I wish so much that someone from their families had come to see Jackie's moment and Jimmy's moment to receive public praise. I wish that Linda's grandmother was here to see her running quickly up to accept the award for most improvement in math. Linda does not look at anyone. Sandy reaches out to pat her on the hand. Linda darts her a brief smile, and then the smile fades back to that disappointed look she had when she realized her grandmother was not coming.

Curt waves the next award in the air for a moment.

"Here's an award for most fluency in reading to Sandy Holton!" Sandy makes her way in her regal manner to the front of the room. The kids don't cheer as loudly for her, except for Jackie, who whistles and yells. Rhonda takes the certificate, looks at it carefully, nods back at me, and puts her hand over Sandy's. Sandy smiles then, not the wide smile that breaks open her face, but a smile that has some nervousness in it, that is more closed, more careful.

Curt calls Mitchell up next, to receive the award for the hardest worker in reading. The kids stomp again, whistle, and cheer. Mitchell dances up to Curt, then playfully snatches the certificate out of Curt's hand. Curt fakes a lunge at Mitchell, then holds out his hand. They slap palms, and Mitchell dances back to his seat, almost ready to start singing. His mother takes the certificate from him and shows it to his little brother, who has been sitting politely beside her during the whole ceremony.

Robert is matter-of-fact about his certificate for most credits earned. The girls giggle, whispering to each other. He's probably the most popular young man in the program, and while he is aware of it, he plays it very cool. He puts his daughter on his lap and lets her hold the certificate.

All of us are fanning ourselves with folded mimeographed programs to keep cool. Small children twist irritably on the creaking metal chairs, but no one disrupts the presentation.

Finally, when Ted stands up to bid everyone a good summer, I hurry to the refrigerator in the teacher's lounge for the cookies, cupcakes, and potato chips. When I return, the ceremony is over. Johnny has loosened his tie. Jackie walks the halls in stocking feet holding her high-heeled shoes. She takes two cupcakes to Jimmy, and they sit together, eating and talking.

Rhonda comes over to me while I am serving punch.

"She reads out loud all the time now."

"I know. She's been reading to me, too," I say, smiling.

"I'm sorry about your brother-in-law and all," says Rhonda, bending close to my ear. She smells good, like lemon soap and lilacs.

"Thank you."

"Don't get too weary," says Rhonda.

Gradually the kids and parents drift out of the room. Jackie doesn't say good-bye but waves as she and Jimmy walk down the stairs together. Before she leaves, Mitchell's mother, Audrey, says thank you to me for my work with her son. I nod and say I am looking forward to seeing Mitchell again in the fall. Linda comes up shyly and gives me a hug. We walk to the top of the stairs, my arm around her waist.

"You take care," I say to her.

She nods, her head down.

"See you in the fall," I say.

"Yeah." She slips away from my arm and walks quickly down to the first floor.

Robert formally shakes my hand. "Thank you, Landsman," he says.

"Good luck, Robert," I say. "Come visit."

"He will," says his mother.

"He will," repeats his little daughter in a solemn voice.

I gather up a few things I want to take home from my room. Ted Marvin stops by the door, briefcase in his hand.

"Have a good summer," he says. "Relax!"

"You have a good one, too." By the time I am ready to leave, almost everyone has gone.

The hallway is quiet. The school has the feel of an abandoned building. Curt guards the stairs to ensure that no one can come back in.

"Will you be back next fall?" I ask him as I walk by.

"Don't know," he says.

"I hope so," I say.

When I get home the house is utterly silent, no one there but me. I like to have this kind of time to myself. I take out a couple of tapes. Aretha Franklin is just right. I want to dance. I dance around and around the living room. This is not a dance of celebration but of urgency. It feels good to get the year out of my body.

JULY

"Great blue Heron
Child in the tallest reeds
standing always alone."

—Gerald Robert Vizenor,
Raising The Moon Vines: Haiku

After a long lunch with a friend, I drive toward downtown to run an errand.

Jackie stands on the corner of Hennepin and Lake. She has obviously lost weight, and her beautiful hair is dyed orange. When I stop the car and wave, she comes over, giving me a quick smile.

"Hey, Landsman." She stands beside the car, looking up the street, pulling on her cigarette. Her cheekbones stand out with each drag. The roundness she had, that surprising softness, is completely gone.

"How you doin'?" I ask.

She shrugs. "Okay. Still work with those old people." She tells me the parts of her life she knows I want to hear.

"You get another job?"

"Not really." She looks around nervously, picks at a pink nail.

"You need a ride somewhere?"

"No. Thanks." She drops her cigarette on the pavement, grinding it out with the toe of her shoe.

"No. I'm waiting on somebody," she repeats.

"You sure?"

"Yeah."

"Where are you living now?"

"Oh, around. Not anywhere all the time."

I scrawl my address on an envelope and hand it to her.

"Here. Write me some stuff." She opens her pink purse and drops my envelope in.

"See you, Landsman." She moves away from my car.

"I hope so," I say, smiling. I wave at her until my hand hurts.

A WEEK-BY-WEEK PLAN: CREATING AN INCLUSIVE COMMUNITY IN THE CLASSROOM

PREPARING TO TEACH
AUGUST

Take time to eat lunch with friends and take as long as you want.

Take time to read some mystery novel you will not feel comfortable reading until the next vacation.

Take time to sleep in, stay up late and watch a movie, go out with friends, and have dinner. Take time to watch the stars with your children.

These and so many other things you do before the craziness of the school year begins are important.

Take time to be alone. This is rare and will certainly disappear when the school year starts in earnest.

CREATING COMMUNITY IN THE CLASSROOM: STUDENT VOICES AS PART OF THE CLASS

The Method

Here is the way I have used short writing activities to create community in the classroom.

1. **I write the topic, or idea, on the board.** For example, "I Am From."
2. **I read aloud a model of this topic,** often a list or a short poem written by someone famous or by a student or a group of students.
3. **I write up my own "I Am From" list as students watch.** I don't necessarily do a whole list but some examples from my own life.
4. **I ask students to write for ten minutes on this topic.** There are some rules for this writing time that I insist on. After the first few exercises, the students insist on them too. It becomes one of those important class rituals and structures that they like because of its pre-dictability. These rules are:
   * *No talking during silent writing time.*
   * *Write what comes into your head, without censoring yourself, or stopping to correct yourself. Just go automatically with thoughts, feelings, or digressions.*
   * *Don't cross out or rewrite, but rather keep the word or sentence you think of first. There will be time later for the revision process.*
   * *Keep your hand moving on the page even if you are writing nonsense for awhile. This hand motion can bring on new thoughts.*
5. **After students have written for ten minutes, I call time. I give them a few more minutes** to finish up their lists, poems, or paragraphs.
6. **I ask each student to read aloud what he or she has written** as we go around the room. Students are always free to pass. I have found, however, that after awhile almost all students want to read aloud. I also have a rule for this reading aloud time:

   No speaking between readers. There will be no comment at all.

The effect of this is that students will write what they feel or what comes to them if they know that no one will say anything afterwards. They need to feel a lack of censorship in order to get to original writing. Later, they may want to mention to someone that they liked a phrase or image that came up, but initially there should be no comment.

This basic method of writing and reading allows students' voices to be the center of the class for a while.

For students who have trouble writing because they are trying to write in a language that is not their original language, the ten minutes allows them to get down at least one or two items or sentences. When it comes their turn to read aloud, I let them *tell* more of what they would have written if they had had enough time.

If students have learning disabilities, I try and sit next to them in case they want help spelling. I encourage these students to get down what they can as well. I also let students with a learning disability *tell* their stories when it is their time in the circle.

On the following pages you will find suggestions for different kinds of activities such as group poems, group read-arounds, response readings, chants, and other ways of using the poetry and prose suggested for the week.

The effect of using these and other activities you create, along with the method above is that you will find you have a class where each student feels he or she is heard, is respected and honored for the unique individual he or she is. This recognition will automatically include the culture from which she comes, the voices from his home he brings, and the celebrations in his or her life.

LATE AUGUST

Thinking Ahead: School begins in a few weeks. Yet it is still summer, still time to plan for overall goals and themes.

Julie Bisson, in her article in *Beyond Heroes and Holidays*, suggests the following antibias goals for the year:

1. Nurture each student's self-identity within the context of a group identity.
2. Promote each student's comfortable intersection with people who are different from them.
3. Foster each student's ability to think critically about bias.
4. Cultivate each student's ability to be an activist and stand up for himself or herself and for others in the face of bias.

Given such goals, you can work in holiday celebrations, family celebrations, and social justice holidays as the year goes on.

What themes are you going to use to provide a center for the year? The choice is limitless:

- Family
- Insider/Outsider
- Courage
- Migrations
- Transformations
- Dreams
- Community

As you plan, what ideas, poems, and activities might fit with what you want to do? Add holidays, celebrations of your own—ones not included here. Let students create their own holidays.

SEPTEMBER

Setting up Your Room

Consult the following publications and books as sources for posters and other decorations for your room. Look in your local stores and newspapers for ideas.

Teaching Tolerance
400 Washington Avenue
Montgomery, AL 36104

Rethinking Schools
1001 East Keefe Avenue
Milwaukee, WI 53212

Beyond Heroes and Holidays
Network of Educators on the Americans (NECA)
PO Box 73038
Washington, DC 20056-3038

Monthly calendars from the year before are also excellent sources of visual art for your classroom. Amnesty International has a fine selection of pictures each year. Look in your local bookstore for images you would like to have on your walls and bulletin boards. Some wonderful multicultural anthologies are available now in bookstores. You can do the same decorating by enlarging quotes from the wise and courageous people writing in these anthologies and have one up in the room each week.

On a more abstract level, consider the neighborhood and/or culture of your students. Drive around. Listen. Taste. Even if you are in a white homogeneous area, students will have different ethnic backgrounds.

Bring in different kinds of music and a small CD player. Listen while you work. Pick out some songs you want to play for your students, as part of a lesson, or simply as they enter and exit your room.

Add pictures, artwork and written work of your students throughout the year, creating a "room of celebration" by June. You do not have to overdo it, but you can add new items as the months go along so that by the end of the school year all students feel as though they are part of the walls and voices of your room.

If you are traveling with a cart because of overcrowding in your school, make a box with pictures, poems, quotes, and artwork on cardboard. You can set them up quickly as the class files in, or pull them out as they relate to the lessons you are teaching.

Question for the week: When do we need independence?
When do we need to acknowledge we are dependent?

SEPTEMBER WEEK 1

Start this week with *Low Risk Activities and Topics* that will let students express themselves yet will not ask them to expose a lot of personal information about themselves.

1. Ask students: Find out how to say "Welcome," or "Welcome to Room [your classroom]" in one other language besides your own. If you have a class of students who speak different languages in their homes, ask them to tell you how to say this "welcome" phrase in their home language. Make posters or strips along the top of the walls with the phrase in each language. Teach students how to pronounce each one.

2. Read aloud from a poem about work or different kinds of jobs. Ask students to talk about what they think it means to work: in school, out in the world each day, after school, on a team, as a friend, as a family member, and around the house. They can do an acrostic poem, finding words they associate with the word work and putting them down the page.

   W
   O
   R
   K

   Ask students to interview a parent or relative or neighbor about their job and talk about what they found out in class.

   Schedule parents to come in each week or two to talk about the work they do.

3. Post or read aloud the following Hmong Proverb as found in the book *Writing Across Cultures*.

"Even a long ladder can never reach the sky. Even a self sufficient person needs the help of others."

Ask students to talk about, or write about what they think this proverb means. How does it apply to their lives?

SEPTEMBER: WEEK 2

Ideas for learning about each other

1. Talk about things that are important to us, both material and emotional. We value our hair, the water, a book, a CD, a smile from our mother or a friend. Ask students to make a list of places they would write their names. Model such a list from your own experience. What means a lot to you? What cannot be replaced? I would put my name on my books, my CDs, my son's forehead, my favorite shirt, the manuscripts of the books I write, my poems. Ask students to read their lists aloud.

2. List the first names of everyone in the class. Ask students to write beside their name four words that describe them. Make a class poem with just the elements students used to describe themselves. Talk with them about what your classroom "contains."

3. Ask students to decide what color fits their spirit. Discuss their choice.

4. Let students make acrostics with their names, listing characteristics about themselves across from each letter.

5. Let students rename themselves. Ask them to tell why they would want a new name.
   Note: Some cultures regard naming and names very seriously. It is wise to keep this in mind when discussing this topic.

SEPTEMBER: WEEK 3

I AM FROM

I am from the piano in my living room
I am from Mexico, the trees are green
I am from apples, I eat them and smell them and they are pretty on trees
I am from the circle of life
I am from Strategy, spending my Saturdays playing games
I am from me and my sister playing tag and going swimming
I am from Martin Luther King's tears
I am from sweet apple pie, which makes me sing to myself!
I am from sewing with my Mom
I am from Bloomington Avenue
I am from lima beans that I hid under the mashed potatoes
I am from a baby girl arriving at the airport dressed in a kimono dress, arms
    outstretched, dark brown eyes
I am from mackerel that I ate every day
    RIGHT NOW I AM FROM AMERICA
    RIGHT NOW I AM AMERICAN

              —students from the Youth Farm in Minneapolis

Based on George Ella Lyons' poem in the book *United States of Poetry*, this is one of the most powerful activities you can do with students: asking them to list all the things they are from.

1. After reading the poem aloud, ask the students to make their own "I am from" lists. Show them a few items of your own to give them the idea: I am from pancakes every Sunday morning, riding horses in Connecticut, weekends in New York listening to jazz. . . .

2. After they are done writing ask students to read their I Am From lists aloud in their entirety, one at a time. Make sure students understand not to make any comments after each person has read, rather allowing for a second or two of silence before moving on to the next person.

3. After everyone has read, including you—the teacher—and any other adults in the room, you might make a comment on the variety you see in the room.

SEPTEMBER: WEEK 4

Group Poem

I am from places

I am from piano that I play

I am from the family of Xiong, which is maybe every where in the world.

I am from an accident waiting to happen

I am from music: the art of sound

I am from my guitar: my six-stringed acoustic guitar with the dove on it. My guitar is a lot older than one, fourteen years older, in fact: but still sounds like my brother's new guitar which he plays only sometimes.

I am from the world at the first time and I am also the first person in the world

I'm from Minnesota: I play baseball

I am from baseball and the old run down fields

I am from a church

I am from the loving warmth of the sun as the trees sway slowly in the wind on a Sunday morning.

I am from a house on the parkway with soft green grass

I am from a big family that loves me.

I am from green bean casserole and clocks.

I am from the yard, from the home, Japan.

I am from the yard, the place I should be

I am from trees and craters with green mosquito nets.

I am from goggles and face masks going down hill with skis, touching the snow and the poles steering me down a hill.

I am from friends and I am the night who is up when morning is sleeping and I am the accident waiting to happen

I am from the park and forest across the street

I am from an accident waiting to happen

I am from he who has brought me here

I am from my neighbors, they like peace and quiet. I am from my neighbors, too bad I am so different

I am from the fear of fell.

I am from places that are unseeable except with my imagination making sense of unsensible worlds.

I am from the night, who is up when morning is sleeping

This is a group poem sixth grade students from Minneapolis wrote one year. In order to construct such a poem, ask each student to circle their favorite line from their own "I Am From" poem. Type one poem using these lines. If possible, print the poem in large type and post it on the wall, like one long poster.

Ask each student to read his her line, going around the room, voice after voice. Or include two lines from students and ask them to go around twice.

You can also ask students to chant in unison "I Am From," followed by each student's individual words. You and your students will think of multiple uses of this poem, including visual art, murals, songs, and dances.

OCTOBER: WEEK 1

I remember dust storms yellow skies. . . .
I remember rainy days through a window. . . .

—Joe Brainerd, from his book: *I Remember*

I remember when I came to the USA
I remember how scared I was
I remember the gun shots when we crossed the border
I remember when a man got killed by a snake
I remember the time that all my family got hurt because we were coming to
   the USA
On top of all that
I remember it as if it was yesterday

—tenth grade student, Minneapolis

1. **Ask students to address a letter** to a friend or family member asking: "Do You Remember . . . ?" This can include songs, fashions, people, cars, foods, events.
2. **Put up a model of your own:** Example: to my sister Lesley: "Do you remember when we ran in and out of the outdoor shower near the ocean and giggled all afternoon? Do you remember when we learned to use hula hoops and you won the contest? Do your remember ice box cookie cake?

   Science teachers can talk about memory: what triggers it? How do memories get into our brains? Why do we remember some things and forget others?
3. **Ask students to create an "I remember" list.** This does not have to be addressed to anyone but is simply a way for them to recall things that happened in their own lives.

   Create a class "I Remember" list. Post it around the room or down a wall. Ask students to add to it as the year goes along, creating a memory board.

I remember things high out of reach. I remember going down to Chicago
   Rainbow Beach
I remember my favorite foods, enchiladas and sachichas roya, the hot salsa and
   tasty beans and cheese.
I remember always hearing my mom telling me to get my butt in before the

street lights came on. I remember walking down the street on Sunday and I could smell the bombest chicken.

I remember when I got my first bike it was a red Schwin. I remember riding it with my best friend for hours around town.

I remember the spring when I knew it was time to start over.

—Part of a 3rd Hour Poem, Work Opportunity Center students, Minneapolis

OCTOBER: WEEK 2

There is a beautiful poem entitled "Indian Children Speak" by Juanita Bell, published in a book entitled *Rethinking Columbus*. In the poem she writes about all the things that people say about Native Americans and then the reality of the children who are Native American and how they are the opposite of the stereotypes she hears about them. Some lines similar to hers might be:

People say African American students don't want to learn
And then Jamal comes into my room, book in hand
Asking about Mozart, Coltrane, velvet pantaloons
Wanting to learn about all he does not know, eyes bright.
People say Latina girls are not serious about getting an education
And then Jennifer comes into my room, rushing to the couch
In the corner, her face buried in a book called *Jane Eyre*, hoping to get an A
On her paper in English Literature
People say Hmong girls are quiet and shy, speaking to each other under their
     breaths
I look over and see Mai Nhia and Sally writing the script to a play
Speaking in prim English, imitating a British Matron, their bodies
Unnaturally stiff. And then they dissolve in laughter, white and Asian.
People say that inner city schools are run down, dumbed down, filled with
Gang bangers. I glance up as my students come in for third hour
And see the way they defy everything that people say,
Asking for missing assignments, settling in for the test I have prepared
Teasing across the room,
And I want to celebrate the wild beauty of their difference.

1. **Ask students to write about a time they felt put down.** This could have been because of their skin color or simply their behavior.
2. **Ask students to write a list poem with the repeating phrase: "people say . . ."** Include examples: "People say teenagers don't want to work hard," (general) "People say my house is run down" (personal).

OCTOBER: WEEK 3

Celebration:

I love life
The Rush I get when I breathe in
The waking and the sleeping
The going and the getting to
The adventures of living

> —Selected verse from poem by Jennifer Jones, Minneapolis student

1. **Ask Students to list small things in their everyday lives they want to celebrate.**
2. **List some of your own:** I want to celebrate the way the light shines in my kitchen, the taste of coffee, the crack in the sidewalk where flowers are growing . . .
3. **Ask students to describe or make a list or discuss the celebrations in their family.**
4. **A class project: Create a class celebration.** Let students think of what they want to celebrate in school that is everyday. Include student poetry, music, and food. Let students create their "Celebration of the Daily" day.

OCTOBER: WEEK 4

A list modeled after Kim Stafford's poem, "A List to Memorize":

Silent things are:
A winter night when it has snowed
The tracks of a deer in the morning
The moment before a baby cries
Sorrow

Loud things are:
The echo of an opera singer
Singing in the Grand Canyon
My mother's anger in the morning
A gunshot near my porch

Things that last forever are:
Summer vacation on the day after school gets out
My brother's loud music
Right after the last breath my grandmother breathed

Class list poem, Sheridan School, Minneapolis:

Silent: Reading quietly to yourself, clowns, writing, sleeping, drawing, thinking
When you talk inside your head it is silent, what I think is silent, mountains are silent dancing

Loud: Fireworks, bombs, a slam from a door, loud music, the bus after school, my Mom yelling, fighting between two best friends, when you can tell someone is sad but they won't admit it, a large truck, someone stomping on a floor, shooting, the roar of distant thunder, a breaking window

Lasts Forever: Family, Brian, Nails, teeth, God, stars, galaxies, pain, love, hair, friendship, plastic, rocks, your first kiss, plastic, metal, sometime friends, bones
A kiss, a letter from someone, especially the alphabet

This is an activity that can be done any time of year.

1. **Ask students to list things one category at a time: silent things, loud things, things that last forever.** Ask them to read after each category so you have gone around three times.
2. **Put together a class list** and ask students to read their own line when it comes up.

NOVEMBER: WEEK 1

Hmong Proverb:
N (Bird) Norque

To Know the seasons listen to the birds sing. To know the folktales
Listen to the old people.

In Class

Warm Up

1. Ask students to **list important people in their lives** from an older
   generation: either relatives, teachers, neighbors.
2. Have them **read their lists aloud.**

Practice

3. **Divide into small groups** (3 or 4)
4. **Ask students to choose one person to interview.**
5. **Have the group prepare questions** to ask this student
6. **Ask them to conduct the interview, asking the questions.** They
   can tape this interview if you would like them to, or they can write
   the answers into spaces on an interview sheet below the questions they
   have devised.

The Interview

7. Ask students to interview someone they know who is older, using the
   same method of devising questions
8. Invite some of these people into your class. Ask the person who inter-
   viewed them to introduce them to the class. Have students prepared
   to ask more questions.
9. After the visit(s) ask students to write about the ways the interview
   affected them in an essay, poem, song, or drawing.

Have a day to "present" these people to another class.

NOVEMBER: WEEK 2

The task that remains is to cope with our interdependence to see ourselves reflected in every other human being and to respect and honor
our differences.

—Melba Patillo Beals, 1994

Windows and Mirrors

Our students love experiences that allow them to look through a window
at those who live differently than they live. Our students need to see themselves in what they do. They need both of these experiences every day.

Window Activities

Ask students to:

Think of someone you see each day, but do not know well.
Imagine a day in his or her life.
Imagine a day in the life of someone with a skin color or culture
or gender that is different from your own.

or

Look at a magazine or newspaper picture of a complete stranger.
Write a series of journal entries as though you were that person.

Mirror Activities

Ask students to make a list of "I believe . . ."
Read these aloud with no comment.
Let discussion happen if it seems constructive.

Ask students to make a list of reasons they think their world is beautiful.
What colors, clothes, foods, and music in their own world add to its beauty?

NOVEMBER: WEEK 3

"If we could find ways of getting people to work on common
projects . . .
racial divisions seem to disappear
and friendships occur."

—Thomas H. Kean, 1997

The whole barrier exists because most people never
come together and sit down at a table . . .
join together, break bread together
And celebrate their differences and their likenesses.

—Oprah Winfrey

There is a whole book devoted to poems about eating entitled: *A Bite to Eat*, published by Redwood Coast Press, 1995, edited by Andrea Alolph, Donald L. Vallis, and Anne F. Walker.

Food is a constant interest of students of any age. It is one way we can reach across cultures and connect with each other. It is another way, too, of telling students that the most ordinary experiences, the most seemingly mundane events, can be the subject of whole poems. Use this week to get students to write about food, their family, their tastes, likes, and dislikes.

Show them lines like these, for example:

"In the morning I smell my father's first cigarette, mixed with the coffee my mother brews, standing at the stove, concentrating on the beginning of the day."

or

"My Uncle Sam knew how to make barbecue sauce so it burned your tongue with its sweetness, almost like you couldn't stand it to be so perfect in your mouth."

or

"In California there is a huge Hmong grocery store. Walking in, I felt like I was back in Laos, in the hills, finding herbs and smelling red flowers in the mist."

Make up some of your own examples.

Language Arts Teachers: To get students started, find some poems about food. Ask students to answer these questions themselves:

Who does the cooking in your family?
What are the sights, sounds, smells, tastes, textures in your kitchen?
Have you ever felt hungry? Write about how it felt. Imagine how it might
    feel if it has not happened to you.

Ask students to write for ten minutes on food.

Science Teachers: Talk about cooking, food, and nutrition.
Social Studies teachers: Talk about food and geography—why some cultures eat certain foods based on where they live.

NOVEMBER: WEEK 4

Cut into lengthwise slices: one earful of darkness
Salt with cold snow—falling at night.
Sing your heart out till you break a window.

—Recipe Poem from book, *Poetry Everywhere*

1. Ask students to look at the following words they find in recipe books: (on board)

   > mix
   > sprinkle
   > dice
   > chop
   > sift

Ask students for more words to add to this list. List them on the board. Ask them also for categories of things we use in cooking:

> Action words (verbs): stir, mix, boil
> Tools (nouns): spoon, knife, sifter, tongs
> Containers (nouns): bowls, pan, cup

Ask them to write a poem or essay using at least one word from all the categories listed.

2. Ask them to think of good music to cook to. Bring it in and play it.
3. Ask them to think of a table ready for the family: the scene, the sights, smells, etc.

   Ask them to describe this scene using all five senses.

   Ask them to describe the people who might be coming, the room, the house or apartment.
4. Ask students to write a recipe for a feast of celebration, or for anything. They may want to write about a birthday, a wedding, a funeral (celebration of someone's life).

   They should be encouraged to do what the recipe poem does: add unusual things and sights and concepts to this poem.
5. Ask students to write a recipe to end world hunger.

   Make it into a class poem.

   Post the poem above a collection sight for donations for food shelves.

DECEMBER: WEEK 1

In Another's Shoes

1. Tell the students you are going to create a story through characters and a celebration (pick a celebration).
2. Give each student a slip of paper with one participant in the celebration listed on it. For example, if the celebration is a wedding, one student will receive a slip that says "Bride" on it. Another will receive "Groom." Another "Best Man." Maybe one for "Jilted Boyfriend of the Bride." Think of enough characters so that each student receives a different slip.
3. Ask students to imagine what his or her character feels about this celebration.
4. Ask them to write a monologue from the point of view of that character.
5. Students should not talk to each other at all about what they are writing.
6. Ask students to read these character monologues aloud. It does not matter if there are a lot of perspectives and thoughts that do not match. This makes for a funny reading. It can also be a moving read around, or one that is silly.

Variations

This activity can be varied any way you may want.
Some ideas:

• Thanksgiving from the point of view of Native Americans, immigrants, or those who are hungry, etc.
• Christmas from the point of view of a Muslim or Jewish family.

This activity is to provide window experiences for some students and mirror experiences for others. You are asking them to empathize.

Another way to approach this would be to ask students to write about an event their family celebrates from multiple points of view. Have the student write a series of monologues from the point of view of different members in his or her own family.

This can also be adapted into a play quite easily. Let students have time to experiment with this activity. They will come up with stage sets, slides, music, and other additions to the original plan.

As a class, invent some holidays or celebrations for the rest of the school year: what do students, as a class, want to celebrate?

> Birthdays
> Winter Solstice
> Little known holidays from other cultures
> Holidays honoring important people in their lives? (mothers, fathers, brothers, friends)
> Holidays honoring music, color, brotherhood, sisterhood?

Let students be inventive and then plan the appropriate celebratory day. Let them bring in music, make posters, write stories, and invite guest speakers to this celebration. Ask them to write poems before the actual day designated around the theme:

> "I want to celebrate music. . . ."
> "I want to celebrate spring. . . ."

If you can find some poems, stories, or essays about the celebration, ask students to read and discuss them. In history, find examples of unusual celebrations.

Ask students to look at your calendar. How would they honor disabled persons? What changes could they advocate to make life easier, create more equity of access for disabled persons?

DECEMBER: WEEK 2

What Is Revolution, Anyway?
Based on Mateo Rose's poem "without fear of being happy"

Revolution is not
> Soldiers with bayonets, men hiding and shooting in the woods
> The smell of gun smoke on a summer night

Revolution is not based on
> Conquering, defeating, squashing
> Beating, winning at any cost

Revolution is
> The unexpected laughter in the middle of a crowded classroom
> The jokes kids make up on winter mornings
>> Irresistible, unstoppable, celebration

Revolution is standing for something as beautiful as peace

In revolution
> A handshake is not giving up
> But rather skin, against skin, a new beginning

And hope is not an illusion
> But what we live on, breathe for, hold close to our hearts

—Julie Landsman

More about Celebration

Ask students to think of the things they want to recognize in their lives: Getting their license, going to the mall alone, the first time they fell in love, their birthday, mother's and father's birthdays, etc. Make a list on the board. Add a few of your own: son's graduation, child going to school for the first time, retirement parties.

Next, have them list what this day is *not*, as in the poem "What Is Revolution, Anyway?"

Example: My first day driving
is not a day to drive during rush hour . . .
is not a day to give all my friends a ride late at night. . . .

Have them list what the day *is*.

> Example: My first day of driving is a day to put the window down,
> feel the wind,
> turn on the radio to KMOJ
> listen to Aretha singing "Respect"

> Our earth is but a small star in the great universe. Yet of it we can make,
> if we choose, a planet unvexed by war, untroubled by hunger or fear,
> undivided by senseless distinctions of race, color or theory.

—Steven Vincent Benet, 194?

In every culture, stories play a central role. The Bible itself is full of stories, and tales were told by storytellers all over the world to pass on information that was never written down at all. Families, too, pass on information to their children by telling stories. From the accounts told by fathers, mothers, grandmothers, and grandfathers, boys and girls learn about another generation, another time in history.

Ask students the questions below to get them thinking about stories they have heard. Then, talk about true stories and made-up ones, fiction and non-fiction, memoir and truth.

If you can, find some "urban myths" to share with students. Ask them to decide whether these myths could be true or not.

Ask students:

1. What are family stories your parents/grandparents/neighbors have passed down to you?
2. What does the neighborhood watcher see?
3. What does the man in the local barbershop know?
4. What can the homeless man who comes into the coffee shop to read the paper tell?

Ask them to:

1. Invent stories or even memories from the point of view of some inanimate objects, i.e., what does the kitchen in their house remember? What stories could it tell of people who lived there years and years ago?

2. What has the street corner seen?
3. What does the river remember?

Ask students to write in prose or poetry stories of these places or others you can think of. Read them aloud.

History Teachers or Geography Teachers: Ask students to make a map showing where their stories come from. Students can write what the river knows, what the mountains have seen. In such a way geography and literature can create an interdisciplinary project around stories that inanimate and animate objects have seen, heard, known.

DECEMBER: WEEK 3

I don't like it when people say we ought to tolerate our differences—I don't buy that. I think we ought to respect and celebrate our differences.

—Bill Clinton, December 3, 1997

First thoughts: This week before a winter holiday is often a restless, nervous, anxious, and joyful time—depending on the student. On these pages, I include ideas for short, fun, and relaxing activities of celebration and anticipation.

I Used to Be But Now

I used to be afraid of the dark, walking down the street alone, the boy next door, my closet, getting lost when my mom went to college and I'd stay with my grand mom and be worried that she won't come home
but now I'm afraid of staying home alone at night when my mom goes on business trips on planes. I think she might crash and die.

I Want

I want to be able to walk across the stage with my hat and gown
I want to make my family proud of me
I want to have the crowd cheer for me

Concrete Poems

In these poems the words are put on the page in such a way that they emphasize the meaning of the poem. In the example below they are in the center of a large piece of paper. They are "all alone" there.

All
A
Lone

Runningalltogetherwegottotheparkanddancedinacircleuntildark.

In this poem the last words: danced in a circle until dark, can be made to form a circle.

Music Lyrics

Bring a favorite song, lyrics typed, and a paragraph describing why you like this song. Ask your students to do the same thing. Play the songs. Pick a line from the song and write from it. Read around what you have written.

Good bye, see you next year when. . . .

Ask students to list the things they want to happen in the next year. List some of what you want as an example: when spring comes early, when everyone studies hard, when my mother's cold gets better, when I learn to bake bread.

WINTER REFLECTIONS: WHEN YOU HAVE A QUIET MOMENT. . . .

Reflect on the principles of Kwanzaa: Unity, Self-Determination, Collective Work and Responsibility, Cooperative Economics, Purpose, Creativity, Faith

Take time for yourself to:

Meditate
  Sing
    Dance
      Read Aloud
        Read silently, curled on a couch, for hours
          Enjoy family and friends

Write a letter to your students and their parents. List the ways you hope to encourage each of the principles of Kwanzaa in your students.

Look over the year so far. What do you want to change? What is working?

Think of rituals or ceremonies or consistent activities that will make the class feel safe for all students.

How will you welcome your students back in January?

      With food?
      With music?
      With color?
      With love?

JANUARY: WEEK 1

As in the days before vacation, the days after vacation should be filled with short, stimulating things to do:

1. Play your favorite music as students come into class.
2. Read "Poetry Should Ride the Bus," found in June Jordan's book *Poetry for the People*, to your students. Choose lines from this poem that will be good ones for writing. Poetry should:
   - "bring hope to your blood"
   - "sing red revolution love songs"
   - "talk about the comins and goins of the world"
3. Or ask students to think of a "_____ should" poem:

   > "Love Should Dance All Night"
   > "Hate should crawl under the porch"
   > "Joy Should Climb a Mountain"

4. Take the same "should" from each student's poem and make a class poem:

   > Fear should. . . .
   > Fear should. . . .

5. Make this poem into a poster and bring it in on Friday to hang up.
6. Have some students beat out a rhythm while others read the poem aloud.
7. Ask students what Winston Churchill might have meant when he said: "The only thing we have to fear is fear itself."

JANUARY: WEEK 2

Outsider/Insider

Ask students to make a list of times they have felt like an outsider:
- first day of school
- new neighborhood
- only one of his or her cultural group or gender at a gathering

Ask students to make a list of times they felt like an insider:
- With their families
- On a sports team

Read examples below or put up some of your own.

Outside

I feel like an outsider because I'm not one of them skinny toothpicks

I feel like an outsider when my little sister starts cursing at me and my mom doesn't do anything about it

I feel like an outsider when my family is going on the fritz

I felt like an outsider when I was abducted and I was on Mars with all these six-eyed freaks

I felt like an outsider when my ex friend invited all my other friends over to her house and left me out

Inside

I feel like an insider when I am not the only girl who likes to play football

I feel like an insider when I am playing football with all my friends from the old neighborhood even though they are all boys

I feel like an insider when there are people I know at a birthday party

I feel like an insider when I am with my friends, when I am in the car, when I am at school, when I am in my apartment, when I am thinking

I feel like an insider when I do something right

Have students read their lists aloud.

Discuss: Who are the **IN CROWD** in the

- Family
- School
- City
- State
- Country
- World
- Universe

JANUARY: WEEK 3

Let the Rain Kiss: Using the chant from Langston Hughes' poem "April Rain Song," help students create poems. Examples include the following:

Let the rain kiss my father so his leg heals faster
Let the rain kiss my mother so she doesn't have to take care of my dad all the
     time
Let the rain drown winter
Let the rain kiss summer
Let the rain drown my dirty room
Let the rain drown mosquitoes

                                        —Sheridan School Students, Minneapolis

Let the rain kiss the dry land and wash away
All the sadness and violence.
Let the rain kiss the mountain so the stream of life will flow
Let the rain kiss the tree's leaves and drip freely on the earth
Let the rain kiss me so I can be clean like water

                                        —High School Student, Minneapolis

Ask students to make their own list of "Let the Rain Kiss" phrases. Read these aloud, this time going around the class one line at a time, so that they keep reading as you go around until all of them have read all their lines.

JANUARY: WEEK 4

The Blues

Come on now why don't you follow my words
because we're almost done, I'll make it easy at first
You got to see
what you want to be
what it means to be the man
with the master plan
Are you the man, now?

—Student poem

I come to the USA
I'm in school every day
I work all the time
taking tests and making rhyme
Then Saturday and Sunday
we do not go to school
That's the best, it's really cool!

—Student poem

Ways to get students started:

1. "I listen to the blues when I get the blues." What does this mean? Is it true for you? Ask students what they think it means to "have the blues." What do they do when they have them?
2. Ask students to look at blues poems. Notice rhyming lines. Ask them to write a blues lyric.
3. Play examples of the blues on a CD player. (BB King, Aretha Franklin, · Al Green, and Eric Clapton are some of the artists the students seem to resonate to.)
4. Let students perform their own blues lyrics, complete with guitars or whatever instruments they need.
5. Invite a musician to come to class to talk about his or her life.

FEBRUARY: WEEK 1

Shakespeare Sonnets

Some random lines:

"When do I count the clock that tells the time
And see the brave day sunk in hideous night, ..." (12)

"Those hours that with gentle work did frame
The lovely gaze where every eye doth dwell. . . ." (5)

"Shall I compare thee to a summer's day?
Thou art more lovely and more temperate" (18)

"The time of year thou mayst in me behold
When yellow leaves, or none, or few do hang
Upon those boughs which shake against the cold
Bare ruin'd choirs where late the sweet birds sang"(73)

At this time of year it is a good idea to let students simply listen to words—all mixed up, older archaic words, new words, words from other languages. This can be fun and gives them a sense of the variety of human speech. I like to read Shakespeare sonnets to students because they are impressed with the rhythm of the words, their difficulty and their beauty.

Find a sonnet you like and read it aloud—one of the great bard's, or a more contemporary one. Then let students try and write their own. You can point out the number of lines for a sonnet, and that the last two lines change the slant of the sonnet, or its meaning, or provide a surprise. They will often get into it if they feel there is a formula to it. Such form provides them with some security.

FEBRUARY: WEEK 2

Playing with Words

Ask students:

1. List words they love. Read these aloud.
2. List words they hate. Read them aloud.
3. Make a collage of words: Choose words or phrases from the newspaper and assemble them on a piece of paper.
4. Scramble words: Ask students to write three sentences. Put each sentence on a strip of paper. After they have done this ask them to cut up the strips, leaving one word only on each small piece of paper. Have them make a pile of their words. Randomly select words from the pile and rewrite these words across a new piece of paper in whatever order they come. Ask them to put in punctuation randomly. Have them read their nonsense sentences aloud. Look for interesting combinations of words. Ask students to type their poems and put them around the room.
5. Questions to get students to loosen up:
   - What is the fastest color? Why?
   - What is the slowest color? Why?
   - If I said I am feeling green today, what would that mean?
   - Why are the blues called the blues and not the purples?
   - How does love walk?
   - How does fear talk?

FEBRUARY: WEEK 3

The sun was gone, but he had left his footprints in the sky. It was the time for sitting on porches beside the road. It was the time to hear things and talk.

—Zora Neale Hurston, *Their Eyes Were Watching God*

Language

Personification

Persona Poem

I am embarrassment	I am love with my jazzy suit
Wearing mismatched shoes	I'm in red and black
Wearing holy clothes	I look so cute, counterattack
Wearing dirty socks	Look what I did
Getting made fun of	took those two kids
Getting yelled at in public	red and black
Anonymous	I dress to attack
	From here there
I am embarrassment	I am everywhere
I live where you live	I eat you up with my sweet perfume
I eat butterflies in your stomach	for vacation I am in Greece
I wear red clothes	where there is a lot of peace
On vacation I go to another person	I'm in love with your life
Sam	No lie

1. List emotions on the board: fear, anger, joy, sadness, loneliness, happiness, crazy. . . .
2. Ask students to add to the list.
3. Tell them to choose one emotion they want to write about.
4. Give them the time to write about the emotion as though this emotion is a person or a place. Have them describe the emotion/person/place in detail—dress, landscaping, etc. Ask them to read aloud. They can also draw their personified emotion to go along with their poems.

FEBRUARY: WEEK 4

"Actions speak louder than words."

1. Ask students to list or act out ways they act to express emotions: fear, love, hate, sadness, pain.
2. List or act out ways their parents express the same emotions.
3. List or act out ways their friends express these emotions.
4. Talk about differences in expression: between generations, cultures, ages, genders, personalities.
5. Ask students to act out an emotion. Ask the class to guess what emotion he or she is acting out.
6. Ask student to write a poem beginning with "Precisely because. . . ." Tell them this poem will most often be about an action they will or will not take.

Put up a model to get them going:

Precisely because I love you too much
I call upon my strength to let you go

Precisely because I like chocolate
I have decided to try and live without it for a week. . . .

Precisely because I am clumsy
I will dance for you to show you how much I love you. . . .

FEBRUARY: EXTRA ACTIVITIES TO GET THROUGH THE WINTER

Protectors

1. Put up the word safe or safety or protectors, or trust, depending on the skill level of the class.
2. Tell the students they are going to make their own acrostics of a word they choose related to safety.
3. Put up a model on the board:

> **P**arents try to
> **R**ead my mind
> **O**nly
> **T**oday they made an
> **E**rror, and thought I
> **C**ould spend the night alone without
> **T**heir company. Wrong!!!

4. Ask students to write their own acrostics. They can use one word for each letter or create a sentence or sentences. Make sure they know the acrostic has to deal with the subject, which is the word itself. "Trust" must spell out words down the side that have to do with trusting, etc.
5. After this exercise, ask them to tell you who they feel their protectors really are. With whom do they feel safest? Do they trust parents, cops, relatives, the president, friends? Why or why not?
6. Ask students to look at this quote from a student:

> My protector is myself. Nobody else, no one, no where.
> I watch my own back
>
> —Minneapolis High School Student

Do they agree or disagree with this for themselves?

MARCH: WEEK 1

Letters

1. Tell students to: Write a letter to someone who has been important to you. Use some of the following phrases to get yourself going:

   • "I like you 'cause . . ."
   • "You are an . . ."
   • "You are . . ."

   Think about how to make this letter into a poem or a song. Ask students to read aloud their letters. Ask them if they want to send these letters on to the person, or would rather keep them for awhile.
2. Ask students to write a letter to a person who is not alive right now but whom they respect or wish they knew.
3. Ask students to write a letter to a famous person whom they would like to know.
4. Ask students to write a Letter to the Editor about an issue that concerns them.
5. Bring envelopes to class and ask students to address one of their letters and send it off. Discuss why letter writing is different from emailing.
6. Describe a telegram to students. Discuss how a telegram uses few words because the sender had to pay for each word. Have students create telegrams.

MARCH: WEEK 2

Creating a Class Character: Introduction

This is an ongoing activity. To begin, ask students to describe themselves or a person they know. They should use the five senses to describe this person, making sure they get a real picture.

- How does the person look?
- How does he or she taste?
- How does he or she feel?
- What does he or she sound like?
- What does he or she smell like?

They can use one word answers or long, anecdotal entries. When they are done, ask them to read aloud what they have written. They can read one "sense" at a time, so you have all the smells at once, then all the sounds of the characters. Or they can read the whole portrait of the person. They can draw the person, bring in or take a photograph of the person, or make a map of where the person lives. This activity can be added to and extended endlessly to build on itself. Science teachers can use it to talk about the human body, the different climates, places, ways that human being react to the place they live in.

Social studies teachers may want to use this activity to discuss the complexity of the lives of all of us—our background, where we live, our genes, etc.—and to emphasize how impossible it is to generalize about a person because of any one factor.

MARCH: WEEK 3

Class Character Continued: Just the Basics, Please

Ask students to work together to create a character. Tell them they will be adding to this description, creating scenes for their character, building conflicts into the character's life as the rest of the year goes on.

In order to get students to focus, ask them to decide on the following about their character. First, have them describe the character by describing the five senses portrait as they did with themselves or someone they knew.

Then ask them to look at the list below and describe their character completely by listing these characteristics:

- Character's name
- Character's nickname
- Sex
- Age
- Education
- Vocation/occupation
- Status and money
- Marital status
- Family, ethnicity
- Relationships
- Places (home, office, car, etc.)
- Possessions
- Recreation, hobbies
- Fears
- Character flaws
- Character strengths
- Pets
- Taste in books, music, etc.
- Correspondence
- Food preferences
- Handwriting
- Astrological sign
- Talents

Variation: Ask students to create two characters together. Or ask them to get in small groups and create a character to present to the class responding to the above list.

MARCH: WEEK 4

Class Character (continued)

Ask students to describe someone they know by describing a room or car or yard that represents this person. In this description they cannot actually describe the person him or herself, but must reveal the person through the details of his or her surroundings:

- What tapes or CDs are around the room?
- What are his or her clothes like?
- Is the room messy or neat?
- What magazines are there? Books?
- Are there musical instruments nearby?
- Sports equipment?
- What is the food in the refrigerator if it is a kitchen?

Ask students to read aloud these descriptions. After each student has read, ask others in the class to guess what this person is like from what they have heard.

- What is his or her age?
- What is his or her personality?
- What does this person enjoy doing?

Now, after you have done this with students, ask them to describe their class character in the same way. Describe his or bedroom, kitchen, yard, car, etc. Gradually students should see the complexity of a person by building this character. Example of one class character:

Basic Facts: Zosha is a woman who lives in Oregon in a house. She is 66. She has a dog named Lisa, who is a golden retriever. She is a retired nurse.

Outside Portrait: She smells like blueberries, apple pie, and fish. She feels like a rubber booth, smooth like glass, soft like the pages of a book. She tastes like apple. She sounds like the ocean soft whisper, like the fish quiet and peaceful, and she looks like fun and she looks yellow.

Inside Portrait: She is thinking: I am planning to go to the beach. I am not afraid of fish. I am thinking of my mother who died long ago.

I am happy like a lark that sings all day. . . .

MARCH: WEEK 5

Events: To create a story using their character, ask students to make a list of possible problems this character can have:

- Can't pay the rent
- Gets in a car accident
- Gets in a fight
- Tells a secret
- Fails a class

1. Ask students to read aloud their own list.
2. Tell them to choose three of these situations they want to put their character into.
3. Put students into three groups. Ask each group to write up a script of their situation and the result. What happens with their character in this situation?
4. Ask them to prepare to act out this situation, to show the class what happens to their character.
5. Let students perform for each other.
6. Create either three one-act plays, or one three-act play to make their character come alive.

Variation (younger grades)

- Day one: Ask students to write three sentences about a character in trouble.
- Day two: Ask students to write three sentences about how their character gets out of trouble.
- Day three: Ask students to draw pictures of the situations they described.
- Day four: Present these scenarios to the class.

APRIL: WEEK 1

Music and Words

1. Ask students to bring in music their family listens to: songs from their mother, father, grandparents, church, celebrations, festivals, etc. For older students, ask them to write down the lyrics of their songs, type them up, and give you (the teacher) the typed lyrics with one paragraph describing the song's meaning for them, their family, or their culture.
2. Plan a celebration day of music and words. Play the songs, discuss the lyrics, and ask each student to talk about the paragraph they have turned in explaining the meaning of this song for them or their family.
3. Look on the Internet for the top 100 songs of the twentieth century. Play these for students, choosing a line from the song to write about. Examples: "Round Midnight," Thelonius Monk (ask students to write about midnight), "Stand by Your Man" Tammy Wynette (ask students to write "hard to be a woman," "hard to be a man").
4. Ask students to write an "I want words . . ." poem. Ask them to think about ways to put their poems to music.
5. Invite a parent or community member to come to class to talk about the importance of music in his or her life.
6. Bring your own song to class one day—not one that you listen to but one that your parents listened to. Put up a timeline on the board showing their age and birthdates, yours, and your students. Talk about how music changes and yet how it lasts.
7. Bring in some songs of protest: "We Shall Overcome," "Ain't Gonna Let Nobody Turn Me Roun'," and others that you find that are current. Ask students to bring in music from their collections that deal with social conditions or issues of importance. Talk about the role of music in history, war, protest, sustaining our lives, and hope.

APRIL: WEEK 2

"I'd Rather . . . Than. . . ."

Here is a very amateurish attempt on my part to write a poem in this pattern
of "I'd Rather . . . Than. . . ." You can use it as a model or make up one
of your own.

I'd rather build a friendship
than watch it fall,
find words to repair it
than lose it once and for all.

I'd die to save my child,
my husband or my friend
I wouldn't die for cars or boats
or money without end

I'd rather walk streets safe at night
than lie behind a gate
I'd rather fight for city life
than live in a place I hate.

1. Ask students to make two lists of risks they have taken: physical and
   emotional. (You can model your own: climbing a mountain, telling a
   friend you feel hurt by something they did, trusting someone with a
   secret, riding a bike twenty-five miles, etc.)
2. Read aloud these lists.
3. Ask students what they feel is worth risking their lives for.
4. Next ask them to look at the above poem. It has a rhythm and rhyme
   scheme like a song (a, b, c, b).
5. Ask students to write their own "I'd Rather . . . Than. . . ." poem
   with rhyme.
6. Finally, if you want, ask them to set the poems to music or rhythm and
   have a performance.

APRIL: WEEK 3

1. Ask students to list things they want to save forever—either personally or on the earth. Below is an example.

Things to Save

Mountains: with white caps
White clouds without grit
Blue behind white behind green
Air of blue behind everything else
Breath

Here is a list I made and put up for my students:

I want to save forever:
My dog Louis,
Clear water,
The Mississippi River Road,
Places in the city to keep homeless people warm,
Beautiful music

2. Encourage students to put everything and anything in the poem: nature, city, objects, private treasures, animals, specific animals, silence, noise, people, etc.
3. Taking from students' lists, make a huge draping poster of all that must be saved.
4. Put it up on Earth Day.
5. Ask students to draw pictures for this, add color and/or music.
6. Maybe even extend this to the school, so that a long list could wind in and out of the hallways of the school, done on shelf paper rolls.
7. Or take your students outside, have them stand behind the list, and spread it out, with two students holding it up.
8. Take a picture, blow it up, put it on the front bulletin board by the office, or send it into the newspaper.

APRIL: WEEK 4

Odes

Traditionally, an ode celebrates something, something small, or even a moment in time. Examples:

Ode to Air

I'm glad you're there
In my ears and under my chair

—Daniel Chaffin, fifth grade

Or combine an ode with an acrostic as in this poem:

Oh! You shine like the moon
Dark yellow like
Everyone has never seen such a

Thing but
Oh! You shine so yellow.

The sun isn't so bright as you.
  Every
Head is watching.
Everybody wants to see you.

Potatoes aren't as good as you.
Oh! Please help the dark yellow
  Potato moon
Trembling with
A
Terrible fright the potatoes keep
  Calling
Oh! Please help bit nobody
  Comes.

—Troy Herman, fourth grade

Ask students to write an ode to one of the things they want to save on the earth. Or ask them to list things they appreciate and write an ode to one. Or ask them to remember small moments, habitual pleasures (e.g., the smell of coffee in the morning); ask them to write an ode to this moment.

MAY: WEEK 1

Leave Taking

Ask students to make a list of times they have left someone or something behind. Provide some examples from your own life:

- First day I went to school
- Saying goodbye to my grandmother when I went away to school
- Leaving Aaron when I went to work each day
- Leaving my parents when I went away to college
- Leaving my students each summer
- When I got married and moved away

Make another list of times someone has left them behind. Again, give students examples from your own life:

- When a boyfriend broke up with me
- When my best friend moved away
- When my parents went on vacations without us
- When my parents went out for dinner or partying and left us home
- When my son went away to school
- When my son got married
- When my favorite aunt died

Ask students to read their lists aloud. Tell them to write down new ones for their own lists as they listen to each other. Sometimes people can remind us of things we thought we had forgotten.

Ask students to write a letter to someone, alive or dead, saying goodbye. In these letters they can use "Do You Remember" lists, if they want. Or they can create new ones for the person they are writing to. If they want, ask them to read these letters aloud.

MAY: WEEK 2

What I Like

Nikki Giovanni has a poem entitled "Knoxville, Tennessee," which begins with the lines:

"I always like
Summer best. . . ."

Students like this line and write some interesting poems around the theme of what they like.

I always like chicken fried,
mashed potatoes made from scratch,
with melted butter
corn,
and some salad on the side

—Minneapolis Student

Ask students to write their own "I Always Like" poems. They can be two lines, six lines, twenty-five lines, or anything in between! Ask them to be specific: foods, neighborhood places, sounds, sights, smells, tastes, how something feels, etc., using the five senses. Give them some examples from your own list:

I always like early morning best, when it is quiet and no one is up
I always like it when my son gives me a big hug at the airport
I always like it when I get to read a book in bed and be lazy all Sunday.

The above poem appeals to students of all abilities as it can be two words to one hundred words.

This poem can be modified to fit holidays or occasions:

I Always Like the Way My Mother. . . .
I Always Like Observing holidays because. . . .
I Always Like Getting Up In The Morning. . . .

You can invent any titles or subjects you want to get students writing.

MAY: WEEK 3

Chants

A chant is a poem that uses repeated lines. It is usually meant to be read aloud. For example:

I come from a city with a thousand words on each corner
Houston, Soho, pretzels, tortillas, delicatessan
I come from a city with a million words in the river
Oil, dockworkers, barges, red windblown cheeks
I come from a city with a multitude of voices at midnight
Jazz saxophone, blues guitar, whimper of a baby before warm milk. . . .

1. Ask students to make a list of things they want to praise: something they admire or that brings pleasure to them and others. Examples: sun, spring, summer vacation, winter, earth, milkshakes, peace, swimming, eating, their family, singing, music. Include some of your own: cooking out, the ocean, the mountains, traveling, walking down the street on the first day of spring, etc.
2. Ask them to think of a praise line.
3. Ask them to write a poem of praise using that line.
4. Go around, asking each student to read aloud his or her poem.
5. Type up the poems and copy them, giving everyone a copy of all the poems.
6. Ask students to read these poems again: have the class reading the chant line, while the author of the poem reads the alternating lines.

Food crackling on the grill [class reads]
Smell of smoke on a summer evening [author reads]
Food Crackling on the grill [class reads]
Kids playing kickball in the street [author reads]
Food Crackling on the grill [class reads]
Don't want to be anywhere else except here [author reads]
Food Crackling on the grill [class reads]

MAY: WEEK 4

Now is the time of year to bring the class together to say goodbye, and to look toward the summer and next year.

1. Ask them to visualize the last day of school.
2. Write a tentative list of things they will do each hour of that day. You can show them your list:
   - 6:00: Alarm goes off
   - 6:10: Alarm goes off again. . . .
   - 6:30: Shower, get breakfast for family with everyone's help
   - 7:15: Head to school
3. Move from this to ask them to think of some things they can do each week of the summer that might be a service to their neighborhood, their parents, grandparents, etc.
4. Make a giant list on the board of all these ideas. Examples:
   - Read to a small child
   - Help an older person take out trash
   - Water plants for Mom or Dad
   - Plant garden on vacant corner of neighborhood
   - Begin college essays for next year
5. Post this list for the rest of the year. Students can add to it and can get ideas off of it. You can even put up phone numbers for students if they want to call and arrange to do volunteer work as a result of seeing this list.
6. You might want to explore summer programs for your students and invite the counselor, social worker, or someone from the neighborhood or country to come in and talk to them about possibilities for the summer, either doing paid work, or camp opportunities, or other volunteer jobs that need doing.

MAY: WEEK 5

1. Ask students to:
   - Think about the history of your family.
   - Make a timeline of your family.
   - Start with the present and go backward.

My birth _____, sister's birth _____

Mother's birth _____, grandmother's birth _____

Put this down the side of the paper vertically so you get a sense of the years passing.

2. Then ask them to list the major events in the lives of people in their family opposite their name, going as far back as they can. Show these timelines to the class, or ask a parent to come in and talk about his or her timeline and the events on it. Or have students find a copy of the front page of a newspaper published on the day they were born. (Libraries will often help you and your students locate this data.) Ask them to find out:

- What events in the world have happened since then?
- What events have you heard about that happened before you were born?

Or ask students to make a list of five ways to bring peace on earth. Ask them to be specific. Combine these into a final wall poster for the year: _____ ways to bring peace on earth. Examples from some of my classes include:

- Work in the neighborhood for better housing
- Stop using words that hurt people
- Make "end shooting violence" posters and give them to everyone on the block to put in their front windows.

JUNE: WEEK 1

3. Read aloud this poem I wrote about a high school where I taught:

Walking Down the Corridor Is Being in Another Country

Freed from first hour,
students pour into the hallway,
hands on hips, some shout:
You tol' her you thought I was with her man last night
you know that's not true.
Others walk by in orange, purple drapes and veils.
In stairwells young men pray and bow—some place to bend toward mecca;
white girls put on make up, spike up their hair with black polished fingernails,
some pull at the rings in their noses and lips.

A hush of Hmong slips through
or maybe louder as a group of girls lets loose
after huddling quiet in the corner all hour.

Five minutes of hip hop,
earphones curved over heads: the latest Puff Daddy.
Some take dreaming steps, tuning into jazz their parents gave them
in the hope it might calm them during afternoons.

Abundance: someone prays and someone sings and someone cries;
one quiet, hungry girl who never knows where she is going
slouches against a corner of the third floor hallway.

Noise thins,
teachers pull doors closed in unison, calling to their students as they might
call to their own children on an early evening in November when
the light has changed, they are worried and want to begin dinner.

Abundance: as a boy speaks quickly, Liberian accent,
as a girl from Somalia slaps palms with her friend
from the Northside of this wild city
as Mexican music comes too loud from the lunch room
where study hall is just beginning.

Silence,
a flat surface of doors.
The young girl who was crying
hurries to the bathroom to be alone.

Hallways
now patrolled by women with walkie talkies,
a buzz from the office

"Fight in the parking lot"
voice back,
"I'm comin, honey, are the cops on their way?"

Hallways
stilled
to two lovers up against the lockers on the second floor, near the science labs;
they laugh deep into the skin of each others' neck,
keep a lookout
and between looks they touch and touch and touch;
at last, they arrange hair and clothes, buttons and lips, drift to class.

After they have gone, silence,
except for a whispered prayer in Somali
as a single delicate boy bends his body toward the eastern sun.

—Julie Landsman

4. Ask students to read the poem this time having different students reading different stanzas
5. Ask students to make a list of what they carry inside them from their other worlds before they even walk in the door to school. What do you bring to class? Joy? Worry? The memory of your grandmother in another country far from where you live? What is in your history, your experience that comes into the classroom with you?
6. Ask students to write an "I have" list that comes from their thinking on what they bring to school. Examples:
   • I have a grandmother who sits at the window all day waiting for me to return
   • I bring an old Hmong ancestor and her fields in Laos when I arrive for class

- I have inside me my grandfather from Connecticut who wore a gold watch with a chain across his vest
- I have inside me a place I spent summers, with surf and sand and blueberry pie
- I have a father who had a temper and scared me when I was little
- I have a mother who list candles every Friday night for Sabbath

7. Ask students to read their poems in couples, alternating stanzas, each reading from their own poem.

8. Let them work on ways to present these poems or dialogue—with music, visual art, photography, or even a play.

9. Remind students that they take with them out of the class, so much from the year combined with their own family history. They have many people inside each of their bodies!

There are years that ask questions, and years that answer.

—Zora Neale Hurston, Their Eyes Were Watching God

SUMMER BREAK: JUNE–AUGUST

Resources and Fine Books

Read at the beach, in your back yard, in the nearest coffee shop or library. Before you read anything else, if you have not read it, read the work of Peggy McIntosh. Her articles are startling and so, so important!

"White Privilege and Male Privilege: A Personal Account of Coming to See Correspondences through Work in Women's Studies." Wellesley, Massachusetts: Center for Research on Women, Wellesley College, 1988.

"White Privilege: Unpacking the Invisible Knapsack." Wellesley Massachusetts: Center for Research on Women, Wellesley College, 1989.

The following are just a very few of hundreds of fine books for adults and young people. I would always suggest that, over the summer, teachers simply read novels written by authors who live in countries and or cultures different from their own. I think I learn as much from novels as I do from factual accounts.

Teaching Tolerance (magazine)
400 Washington Avenue
Montgomery, AL 36104

Rethinking Schools (Journal)
1001 East Keefe Avenue
Milwaukee, WI, 53212

Rethinking the Classroom (Vol. 1, 2)
1001 East Keefe Avenue
Milwaukee, WI, 53212

Beyond Heroes and Holidays
A Practical to K–12 Anti-Racist, Multicultural Education and Staff Development
Network of Educators on the Americas (NECA)
PO Box 73038
Washington, DC 20056–3038

Reading, Writing and Rising Up (Teaching Writing)
Rethinking Schools
1001 East Keefe Avenue
Milwaukee, WI, 53212

Why Are All the Black Kids Sitting at Separate Tables in the Cafeteria?
Beverly Tatum

Seeding the Process of Multicultural Education
(a selection of readings and first person accounts)
Cathy Nelson and Kim Wilson, editors
Minnesota Inclusiveness Program

Teaching for Change
Best K–College Resources on Equity and Social Justice
(catalogue)
www.teachingforchange.org

A Hope in the Unseen
(journalist account of one young man's journey from Washington, DC, to
    Brown University)
Susskind

And Still We Rise
(journalist account of a year at an inner-city LA School gifted program)
Miles Corwin

Their Eyes Were Watching God
(novel: high school)
Zora Neale Hurston

Monkey Bridge
(novel: high School)
Lan Dao

Seedfolks
(novel: middle school)
Paul Fleischman

The Skin I'm In
(novel: middle school)
Sharon G. Flake

Perma Red
(novel: high school)
Deborah Magpie Earling

Coming of Age in America: A Multicultural Anthology
Frosch, editor

Welcome to Your Life: Writings for the Heart of Young America
(anthology: high school)
David Haynes, Julie Landsman, editors

Braided Lives: An Anthology of Multicultural American Writing
Minnesota Humanities Commission

Always Running, Memoir
Luis j. Rodriguez
Simon & Schuster

Makes Me Wanna Holler
(memoir)
Nathan McColl

Make Lemonade
(novel)
Virginia Euwer Wolff

Unsettling America
(an anthology of multicultural poetry)
Gillan and Gillan, editors

That Kind of Sleep
Poems by Susan Atefat-Peckham

AFTERWORD

So many people have asked me what became of the young people I describe in this book. As I said in the original introduction, their names were changed and some details of their life were also changed. I could not find them all after the book finally came together and did not want them to be easily recognizable for many reasons having to do with their own safety.

The character Sandy is based upon went on to graduate. Jackie was based on two young women, one went on to marry and live in a suburb, the other returned to the street and got caught up in the drug trade. Jimmy completed two years of high school. Johnny also went on to the rest of his high school career. I believe he got his GED degree.

I see students like these students everywhere now. There are few programs for them, but rather they are "mainstreamed" into regular classrooms with some Special Education assistance in the case of those with learning disabilities. They are often lost, drop out or simply disappear from the education radar in the city in which they live. I see them, though, at check-out counters working for minimum wage, in restaurants, in schools for troubled students as aides in the classroom, or even teachers. Their potential is without limit. They are bright young people. For awhile their lives may be in crisis, or they may come from homes that are as stable as my own two parent home in Connecticut during my adolescent years. There is no classification, no generalization that can encompass them in all their complexity, just as racial and ethnic generalizations never work to describe the vibrant and remarkable individuals in our schools. They are simply kids, who, for whatever reason, have lost their way for a while.

I have noticed, since this book was published ten years ago, that there is a tendency on the part of those who do not know these young people individually, to give up on them, write them off, or discount them quickly. I believe we were a more open, compassionate country when *Basic Needs* came out than we are today. And make no mistake about it, these young men and women pick up on such rejection with great immediacy. They lose hope, become cynical, or despondent and develop a dangerous recklessness. Yet, as quickly as this happens, just as quickly they can be motivated, encouraged and given hope again. With time, attention, compassionate teachers and small groups in which to connect with meaningful adults in their lives, they can become important sources of good in our communities. If we fund our schools decently, if we lower class sizes, find great counselors and artists, poets and accountants to bring into the classrooms who look like the young people, they will have a personal connection to worlds and possibilities they never dreamed of before.

It is with great happiness that I see this book reprinted. Maybe, like my father (a conservative man who believed solely in boot strap progress even without the boots), those who read *Basic Needs* will feel, as he did, "I just can't write off those punks on the corner any longer since I read your book. Gotta admit that, Julie."

May we look at each young man or woman on the corner with great generosity, mercy, and hope. May we take them into our classrooms, our lives, and our hearts. And more important, may we never give up on them, even at nineteen, even at twenty-one, even at forty-five. There is the capability for redemption in them and in ourselves as well.

ABOUT THE AUTHOR

Born in Connecticut, **Julie Landsman** received her B.A. from George Washington University, her teacher's certification from Carleton College, and her certification in special education from the University of Minnesota in Minneapolis. Landsman, an educator, writer, and writing teacher, has been a teacher and behavior specialist in inner-city and suburban schools in the Minneapolis Public School system for more than twenty years, working in special settings for students with academic and behavioral problems.

She is a frequent speaker and has had many essays and poems published in journals such as Artpaper, the Hungry Mind Review, and Hurricane Alice. In 1985, Landsman won the Creative Non-Fiction Contest from the Loft, in 1986 she won the Loft McKnight Award for prose, in 1989 she received a Minnesota State Arts Board Grant, and in both 1990 and 1991 she received a Jerome Foundation Travel Grant.